Winning Debates

Winning Debates

A Guide to Debating in the Style of the World Universities Debating Championships

Steven L. Johnson

International Debate Education Association

New York*Amsterdam*Brussels

For Jen and Mamie

Published by:

International Debate Education Association

400 West 59th Street

New York, NY 10019

Library of Congress Cataloging-in-Publication Data

Johnson, Steven L., 1968-

  Winning debates : a guide to debating in the style of the world universities debating

championships / Steven L. Johnson.

     p. cm.

  ISBN 978-1-932716-51-1

  1. Debates and debating. I. Title.

  PN4181.J545 2009

  808.53–dc22

                              2009007972

Design by Gustavo Stecher and Juan Pablo Tredicce | imagenHB.com

Printed in the USA

 IDEBATE PRESS

Contents

INTRODUCTION

On Winning

I'm frequently asked what it takes to win debates. The answer is deceptively simple: winning debates requires merely that you persuade your audience that you've won.

The good news is that we are well practiced in persuading others. Nearly every day (and some scholars would say with every word we utter—more on this later) we try to change what someone else thinks or does. When we ask someone to go to lunch with us, when we offer our opinion on some issue of the day, when we try to convince a teacher to reconsider a grade on an assignment, and in hundreds of other small examples we are engaged in persuasion. You have been persuading people all your life.

The bad news is that debating focuses a bright light on these persuasive efforts and subjects them to the scrutiny of critique and adjudication. Rather than simply measuring the success of your efforts to persuade by whether or not the person with whom you're speaking goes to lunch with you, in debating you are pitted against others whose exclusive goal is to prevent you from getting what you want. Moreover, someone listens to your persuasive efforts and ranks them relative to those with whom you're engaged. You have limited time to persuade those making the decision—no longer, for example, can you wear someone down with continued requests (a tactic favored by children in their efforts to persuade parents). And you must persuade on a topic that someone else gave you—you don't necessarily get to choose which side of an issue you defend.

Even with all those challenges (or, perhaps, because of them) debating remains one of the best ways to hone the skills of persuasion. Like anything, you get better the more you do it; debating provides abundant opportunities to become a better persuader.

This book, then, is focused on how to get the most out of the experience of debating. My belief—one reinforced by my experience as a debater, coach, and adjudicator—is that the academic exercise of debating is extraordinarily powerful because of the competitive motivations of those engaged in it. Debaters want to win debate rounds; they have, therefore, an intrinsic and compelling reason to learn to persuade more effectively. One of my goals is to offer perspectives, strategies, and tactics that will help debaters to be more effective persuaders and, therefore, to win more rounds. Put simply, I want to offer you the tools for winning debates.

But an equally important, second goal is to improve the practice of debating itself. In the same way that any competition pushes its competitors to excellence, debating gives its participants the chance to transcend. The art of persuasion (and it is an art—one of the first arts studied by the ancient Greeks and Romans, the founders of Western thought) offers its practitioners the opportunity to go beyond the average and ordinary of human experience, to pursue the sublime. Good debaters are artists, and the debates they create are works of art. Like all art, debating demonstrates the potential of human beings to create excellence. Good debating, like the creation of good art, reveals and illuminates the human experience. Debating can be beautiful; I hope that this book in some small way contributes to producing debates that are intriguing, compelling, and inspiring. In other words, I want to promote more "winning" debates.

To achieve these two goals, I'll begin by exploring a perspective on argument that has always helped me explain what is required of a successful debater. Chapter 1 lays out a philosophy of argument that provides insight into how people think about the arguments they encounter in a debate round and, therefore, how you can construct those arguments (as a fortunate coincidence, this philosophy also explains a lot about how human beings think outside of debate rounds).

From there we'll take on the much larger task of laying out the practice that emanates from this philosophy. The remainder (and the majority) of this book will be devoted to identifying the skills necessary to win debates and offering ways to develop those skills.

Chapters 2 and 3 outline the "language" of debating — argumentation — by discussing what an argument is and how those arguments interact, both logically (in different modes of argumentation) and structurally (through points of stasis).

Chapters 4 and 5 focus on the techniques of debating and the format in which those techniques may be exercised. Chapter 4 introduces three foundational skills all debaters must master: constructive argumentation, deconstructive argumentation, and the framing of arguments. Chapter 5 examines the format of British Parliamentary debating and describes the roles of the speakers who participate in that competitive format.

Chapters 6, 7, and 8 offer an advanced perspective on debating designed to challenge and inspire seasoned debaters while offering insight for novice debaters. Chapter 6 examines a perspective on human decision making and applies that perspective to academic debating. Chapter 7 offers a number of paradoxical observations about debating designed to promote reflective thought about the best practices of debating. Chapter 8 outlines a few of the advanced tactics I've found particularly useful when coaching my team.

The text concludes with a discussion of adjudicating debates in Chapter 9. While written to guide adjudicators in the practice of calling debates, this chapter will also be of great interest to any debater who may benefit from knowing how adjudicators think about rounds.

In all, I hope the text provides a coherent, useful vision of debating that will encourage discussion, disagreement, and experimentation from all of us involved in the activity. When we search out ways to move the practice of debating forward, we are—by definition—involved in winning debates.

CHAPTER 1

A Philosophy of Debating

The Foundations of a Philosophy of Debating

When asked, most people would likely say they prefer to avoid arguments. Arguments, they would probably note, are the source of much pain and frustration in our interactions with others. Given most people's understanding of arguments, this point of view is not surprising.

It seems odd, then, that there exists a long tradition in Western educational systems of teaching people how to argue. Do the teachers in these schools want their students to suffer? Not at all. In fact, the preeminent place given argument in Western educational traditions is grounded in a vision of argument not as an unpleasant consequence of human interaction but as the very foundation of human knowledge.

Humans' knowledge of the world around them is the product of their interpretation of their experience. A significant difference between humans and other creatures is the ability to interpret our experiences in a variety of ways; for humans, experience is not fixed but is the product of the choices we make.

Animals interact with the world instinctively; they encounter stimuli from the environment around them and react according to their biological "programming." For example, driven by a genetic motive beyond their comprehension, animals mate neither for the joy of the act nor for the beauty of the relationship but simply to satisfy a biological urge to procreate.

Humans, on the other hand, are not limited to knowing the world only through their instincts. In order to interact with the world around them, human beings first construct the meaning of their experiences through the words they use to describe that world. In fact, because they attempt to assign meaning to the world around them, humans are largely removed from instinctive ways of knowing. Rather than simply satisfying biological urges by mating with the first available member of their species, for example, human beings construct elaborate symbolic rituals to explain mating: love, courtship, fidelity, marriage, and divorce are but a few of the myriad constructs created by humans to explain their romantic involvement with others.

Rhetorical theorist Kenneth Burke explains people's need to construct the meaning of their world by calling human beings "symbol using animals." Burke intended to convey that the distinguishing characteristic of humans is their use of symbols—language—to explain their experiences. Burke believed that humans are both blessed with and cursed by their ability to interpret their experiences: on the one hand, humans are free to construct elaborate, often beautiful, and ultimately satisfying explanations of the world around them. On the other hand, the freedom to construct the meaning of our world also means that there is not *one, correct, absolute* interpretation of that world.[1]

Humans are required to operate in a world of limited and imperfect information and, therefore, limited and imperfect perceptions. Because we construct our world through the symbols we use, we know that our explanations are our own creations. Because we know that we created these explanations—and that others may create different explanations—we are constantly unsure of the meaning of our experiences. Uncertainty Reduction Theory explains that human beings communicate with each other to reduce uncertainty about the world around them that results from a lack of fixed meaning.[2]

Three observations may be made about the relationship between uncertainty and communication:

1. Uncertainty is pervasive. Because human beings are separated from instinctive experiences of the world and create meaning through their use of symbols to describe their world, uncertainty is the hallmark of the human experience. In other words, until we interpret our experiences (and sometimes even after we arrive at an interpretation), we're uncertain about what our experiences mean.

2. We reduce our uncertainty through communication. While we are capable of assigning meaning to our own experiences, we become more certain about our own interpretations of the world when those interpretations are confirmed by others. When we share our interpretations of the world around us with others and they respond (by affirming, denying, or offering alternate interpretations), we are working to reduce the uncertainty of raw experience. We may also rely on others to interpret experiences for us, thereby reducing our uncertainty.

3. The desire for certainty is compelling. Humans don't like to experience uncertainty and will act to reduce their uncertainty about their world. The reduction of uncertainty is a strong motivating force. We are compelled, therefore, to communicate with others to reduce our own uncertainty.

If uncertainty, and the insecurity that results from it, is pervasive and compelling for individual humans, imagine the motivation generated by the collective uncertainty of a group of people when faced with a new, undefined experience. No instinct can tell a nation whether a belligerent neighboring state poses a legitimate threat to national security or whether the benefits of developing a natural resource outweigh the inevitable environmental consequences of that development. In such circumstances, *our collective understanding is created through the communication we share.*

French philosopher Michel Foucault recognized that the process of communication — particularly among members of a society — not only creates the meaning of our experiences but also distributes power to those able to create and control the meaning of experience.[3] According to Foucault, through our communication about our collective experience we create *discursive formations.* Discursive formations are systems of interpretation and meaning created through shared discourse that guide and constrain a culture's interactions.

For example, the laws of a society are discursive formations. Those laws provide certain protections and seek to limit certain behaviors, yet they are little more than a record of communication between members of that society. In Western liberal democracies, laws are typically the product of a legislative system in which the desirability of a particular course of action is discussed and debated. A decision by the deliberative body or the population at large is reached and, if the proposal is successful, that conclusion is recorded as a law. That law then becomes available to the state as a means of controlling its citizens' behavior.

Foucault's interest in discursive formations grew mainly from his recognition that the power in a society — that is, the capacity to control others — is determined in large part by the ability to define and manipulate discursive formations. Put simply, if you control the description of an experience, you control that experience and the people involved in it. Consider the difference between the interpretations of two recent tragic events in American history.

On April 15, 1995 a rented truck loaded with explosives was detonated in front of the Alfred P. Murrah federal building in Oklahoma City, Oklahoma. Over 160 people died in the resulting blast. Timothy McVeigh and Terry Nichols were tried and punished for their involvement in the incident. At their trial, federal prosecutors asserted that the motivation for the attack was retaliation for policies of the U.S. government with which McVeigh and Nichols disagreed.

On September 11, 2001 coordinated attacks on the World Trade Center in New York City and the Pentagon in Washington, DC, and the grounding of a hijacked plane in Shanksville, Pennsylvania took the lives of nearly 3,000 people. Attributed to al-Qaeda, a fundamentalist Islamic group, the September 11 attacks were allegedly carried out as retaliation for U.S. foreign policy.

These two events — the two largest terrorist attacks ever on U.S. soil — illustrate well the power of choosing language to interpret experience. Both events were terrorist attacks motivated by frustration with U.S. policy. Both resulted in the deaths of innocent civilians and dramatically changed how American citizens thought of themselves and their security. The difference between the events and, more importantly, the consequence of those events lies in the words we use to describe them.

The Oklahoma City attacks were largely described as a criminal act. The governmental response was focused on identifying and prosecuting the alleged perpetrators of the crime. The resulting trial, verdict, and punishment seemed to provide a degree of closure for the country. September 11, on the other hand, was interpreted as an act of war. Those who participated in the attack and their supporting organization were identified as enemies of the state. A full-blown invasion of a nation alleged to support the al-Qaeda organization was staged, and the resulting Global War on Terror is ongoing.

The two very different interpretations of these two fundamentally similar events were the product of the language used to describe them: in one case, the "official" response was to identify the act as a crime; in the other, the attack was described as an act of war. The seemingly simple decision of what to call these events had (and continues to have) a profound impact on the lives of people around the world. The interpretation of these events set the stage for either a discreet response to a violation of law or an on-going military action that has lasted years, killed thousands, and cost billions of dollars.

Clearly, how we choose to interpret our reality affects us. How, then, do these interpretations come into being? How are they created and spread? How does an entire society come to regard one attack as a crime and another as an act of war? If language choice does the work of initially describing these events, then arguments are responsible for convincing others to accept these descriptions.

Reduced to its essential function, an argument is simply a proposed interpretation of some experience backed by reasons for that proposed interpretation. An argument presents a claim—about what something is, about what relationship exists between things, or what value something has—and then offers reasons others should accept that interpretation. We experience something and, because we desire certainty, we present an argument to others that establishes how we think that experience should be interpreted.

While we're making arguments for our perspective, we may encounter others who have different interpretations of the same events and, therefore, different arguments to justify their interpretations. Our arguments are then tested by others' arguments: our audience is asked to choose (or decides to choose) between these competing descriptions. In the end, the interpretations our audiences find most compelling win out and are accepted as the standard interpretation of that experience.[4]

Of course, these interactions seldom proceed along such clear lines. Often it's not clear what someone is arguing or what interpretation they want us to accept. Moreover, we may not know when or if a particular perspective "wins" over another; a winner is seldom declared outside of formal deliberative settings (like legislative or judicial bodies — or debate rounds). Instead, we attempt to convince others and are satisfied if some seem to come to our point of view.

Regardless of whether our persuasive efforts are concluded formally or informally, in the end we realize that our perceptions are our own and that the others with whom we interact will have (and, despite our best efforts, may continue to have) their own. We realize that our interpretations are not fixed, absolute, or objectively verifiable; they are the product of our imagination and our ability to use language to convince others that our interpretations are valid.

A Philosophy of Debating

From these observations about how humans use arguments to construct their reality, we can extract a philosophical framework that illuminates the practice of debating. This philosophy may be expressed in two premises and a conclusion:

Premise 1: Debate is a contest of interpretations and, therefore, arguments.

Debating requires participants to persuade an audience about the truth or falsity of the motion; it is a contest of the arguments used to prove or disprove that motion. The goal of both teams engaged in the debate is to offer an interpretation of certain events that leads an adjudicator to accept or reject the motion under consideration. In this way, the arguments used in a debate round are no different than those used outside of the round. Therefore, the same qualities that make a proposed interpretation of an experience compelling outside of a debate round should make an argument in a round compelling. We'll spend a lot of time in the remainder of this book discussing those qualities and how to create arguments that display those qualities.

Premise 2: Evaluation of arguments is a subjective activity.

Like any effort to persuade, the success of the arguments in debates depends entirely on the perception of the audience: if the adjudicator prefers your argument to your opponents' you will likely win.

The complication, of course, is that what makes your arguments preferable to one adjudicator may not make them preferable to another. What one adjudicator may find a gripping explanation of some position another judge may believe strains credibility.

That said, there are some approaches to argument that most recognize as excellent. Even more importantly, there are typical approaches that an opposing team may employ to test their opponents' arguments and to identify (for the adjudicators) their flaws.

Nonetheless, persuasion is a fundamentally human activity and, as such, it will always be imperfect and mysterious. You will frequently make arguments that you believe are outstanding. You will make claims and offer proof that you believe are much better than your opponents'. You will offer critiques of your opponents' arguments that you believe devastate their overall effort to prove their position. You will compare your arguments to your opponents' and to the motion and will demonstrate clearly that your efforts are superior. And you will still lose.

Part of what debate teaches is that you can't always understand or successfully influence the perceptions of those around you. You will have to find peace with decisions people make. As hard as it may be when this happens, in many ways this is one of the most valuable lessons debating can teach.

These two premises lead to a conclusion that will inform the remainder of this book:

Conclusion: There is no "right" way to debate.

The premises sound decidedly negative. To say that debate is a contest of competing interpretations of reality and that we can never know with certainty why one person prefers one argument to another sounds like a condemnation of the activity. Quite the opposite.

These very same observations are what make debate such a rich and rewarding competitive and educational exercise. It is debating's subjectivity that makes it such a challenging and valuable activity. In debate, the very rules by which the contest is evaluated are subject to the persuasive efforts of the participants.

Unlike other contests, debating has few rules that are fixed. Speaker order and time limits are good examples of the rules that do exist in academic debating: the rules that do exist tend to be those that govern how each round will be administered.

Substantive rules—that is, rules governing the *content* of debates—are virtually non-existent. On its face, this isn't that earth shaking: because the topics of debates change regularly, it would be nearly impossible to define what may and what may not be said by the competitors. Moreover, the very nature of debate as an exercise in free expression recoils at the notion of restricting what may and may not be said in a round.

But this absence of substantive rules also means that the very standards by which the adjudicators will determine the winner of a particular round of debate are legitimate subjects of debate. Should an adjudicator pay more attention to the effects of a proposal on the liberties of a country's individual citizens or the collective security of the nation as a whole? Should an adjudicator give more consideration to the environmental concerns of implementing a policy or the economic gains that will result from passing the policy? These decisions—the very decisions that the adjudicator will have to make to determine who wins the round—are subject to the debaters' arguments.

Moreover, there is little that is expressly prohibited as strategy in debating—since most strategy is rooted in the content of the arguments made in pursuit of that strategy. Can a debater make reference to his or her own personal experience? May an Opposition team offer an alternate policy proposal to counter the desirability of the Proposition's policy? Can a team argue that while the advocacy of the opposing team may be true, the broader consequences of voting for their position cannot be tolerated?

If asked as inquiries about what is "permitted" in debate, these questions are fundamentally flawed. Rather than asking if something is *allowed* by some imagined rules, debaters should ask instead: "Is this approach strategically advantageous?" In more simple terms, if what you're doing helps you convince the adjudicators, then the approach is appropriate.[5]

The lack of a "correct" approach — both in terms of what will persuade a judge and in terms of what the rules permit — creates a great deal of uncertainty that is often met by novice debaters (and adjudicators) with a longing for clearly defined rules and standards. To satisfy this longing — that is, to attempt to legislate and standardize the content and practice of debating — would be much like demanding that we identify one way to paint or a standard way to play music. To do so would be contrary to the very nature of the activity. As a subjective, human activity, debating is an act of creation: the debater makes choices about what to say, how to say it, or what relevance that utterance is given in the round. These choices reveal (and construct) who that debater is; like any art created by any artist, they are the creative expression of that debater. What makes art and music wonderful is their diversity: the beauty of art lies in the unique interaction between artist and observer; the enchantment of music is in the uniqueness of expression of the composer or musician. Debate is no different.

In this book, I do not recommend one way to debate. Instead, I hope to present a variety of tools that, when used alone or in concert with others, may increase the chances that you will win the round. Learning to choose the most effective tactics for a particular situation is in many ways far more important than familiarity with the tactic itself. When you master both you will be well on your way to winning debates.

CHAPTER 2

Arguments and Argumentation

When many people think of an argument, they imagine a dispute between individuals. Often thought to be unpleasant, argument — as most people imagine it — may involve anything from a polite difference of opinion to a screaming match between bitter rivals.

In the context of debate, none of these conceptions of argument is accurate. Here an argument is the fundamental building block of persuasion. *An argument is a collection of statements organized in a way that highlights connections between those ideas to demonstrate that because some of the statements in the collection are believed to be true, other statements in the collection should be accepted as true.*

The Elements of Argument

Arguments are composed of three components: *claim, support*, and *inference*. The *claim* is the statement that the person making the argument wants the person hearing the argument to accept. If I offer an argument that seeks to demonstrate that euthanasia should be permitted for terminally ill people, the claim that I want you to accept is "the state should permit euthanasia of terminally ill people." Claims are the ideas that the audience does not yet accept as true and which the person creating the arguments seeks to have the audience accept.

By itself, however, a claim is not an argument. For example, if presented with only the claim that euthanasia should be made legal, most people would ask "why?" To motivate the audience to accept the claim requires that the person advancing the argument present support for that claim.

In an argument, *support* is an idea or set of ideas the audience accepts as true and that provides foundation for acceptance of the claim. The person making the argument hopes to move the audience from what they believe (the support) to what they don't yet believe (the claim). In the euthanasia argument, the arguer may offer as support the idea that upon death, the terminally ill patient's physical suffering ceases. Provided the audience accepts this support, they may connect it to the claim that euthanasia should be legalized.

The true magic of argument happens when the audience discovers the connection between claim and support. The discovery of this connection is known as *inference*. In our euthanasia example, the connection the audience would discover is that since death ends physical suffering and euthanasia hastens the inevitable death of a terminally ill person, euthanasia is desirable. This desirability, expressed in terms of a society's public policy, becomes a reason for the legalization of euthanasia.

The process of inference — of realizing the relationship between ideas — is the force that moves the audience from what they believe (the support) to what we want them to accept (the claim). Whether made explicit by the arguer (through an explanation of the relationship that exists) or left to the audience to discover (through their own rational process), inference is the engine of argument.

Regardless of how inference is activated by an argument, however, some standard approaches to structuring ideas exist among differing arguments.

Forms of Argument

Arguments take a variety of forms. The most basic form, addressed in our euthanasia example, is known as a **simple model** of argument.

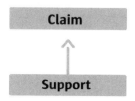

In this model, the support is below the claim, indicating that the support acts as the foundation for the argument. The arrow indicates the inference, or the movement of the audience's belief from the support (in which they believe) to the claim (in which they don't yet believe). The argument for legalizing euthanasia would look like this:

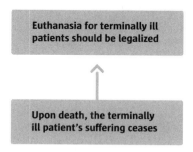

Few arguments are as straightforward as the simple model suggests. Instead, the statements that make up most argument may serve various and sometimes multiple functions. Some variations on the simple model of argument follow.

The **chain model** of argument recognizes that an arguer is seldom certain what his audience believes and, therefore, cannot be sure which ideas will function as support. Perhaps that which the arguer thinks is support for a particular claim may itself become a claim for which the audience demands support.

In the debate above, for example, an arguer may say that euthanasia should be legalized (the claim) because an individual's right to choose to die should be respected above all other concerns (the support). It's possible, however, that an audience wouldn't believe that the patient's right to choose is paramount, insisting that the family and the larger society have a stake in that person's decision. If that's the case, the support offered becomes a claim to be proved.

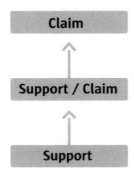

In the case of the euthanasia argument, the arguer may attempt to substantiate the support by arguing that an individual's autonomy in decision making is essential to his humanity. Such an argument may look like this:

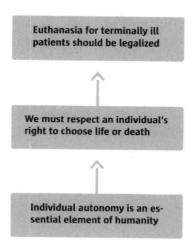

In other cases, the arguer may offer a variety of bases of support as foundation for his claim. Providing a variety of support for the claim increases the chances that an audience will find compelling at least one and perhaps multiple areas of support. This form of argument is represented in the **cluster model**.

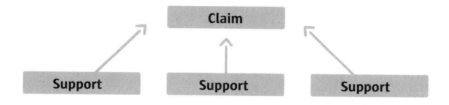

In the euthanasia example, the arguer may claim that euthanasia should be legalized because allowing euthanasia ends the suffering of the terminally ill; because allowing euthanasia honors the individual's autonomy in making his or her own decision; and because legalized euthanasia will avoid the considerable expense of caring for a terminally ill patient.

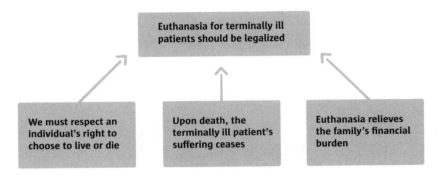

Finally, the **complex model** of argument represents the combination of the chain and cluster models. This form occurs when the arguer offers a variety of bases of support for the claim, some or all of which may themselves become claims that need supporting. Most arguments resemble the complex model.

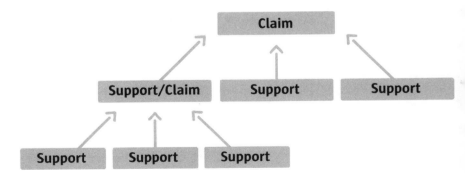

If all the versions of the preceding arguments about euthanasia were combined, they would form a complex argument:

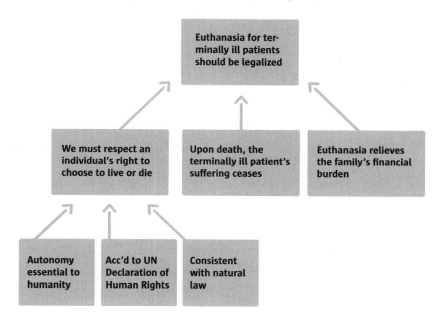

Argumentation

Arguments are to argumentation as sentences are to conversation. In both cases, the activity (argumentation or conversation) requires the elements (arguments or sentences), but the elements alone are not sufficient to constitute the activity. In other words, you can have arguments without having argumentation; you can speak sentences without engaging in conversation.

Argumentation occurs when at least two individuals advance, critique, and defend arguments in an effort to prove that their claims should be preferred to the other arguer's claims. This exchange requires the participants to develop and articulate their own arguments, to listen to the arguments of the other participant(s), to critique the arguments made by the other participant(s), to defend their own arguments against critique, and to compare and contrast the arguments made by all the participants in the exchange.

If I were to offer the argument about euthanasia outlined above and you presented an argument against the legalization of euthanasia, we would be engaged in argumentation. Argumentation may take place with the goal of convincing those who argue to change their actions or opinions, or it may seek to convince an audience to change their actions or opinions. Debating is a structured form of argumentation that seeks to convince an audience of a particular point of view.

Modes of Argumentation

Argumentation occurs over a remarkable variety of subjects and takes a remarkable variety of forms. There are, however, some predictable and identifiable types of argumentation that arise time and again, particularly in competitive academic debating. These themes, determined by the subject and focus of the argumentation, are known as *modes of argumentation*. Understanding modes of argumentation helps us to know which arguments are relevant in a particular disagreement, what support is needed to prove a claim true, and how opposing claims may be countered.

Through a consideration of the types of arguments typically encountered in debates, argumentation scholar Robert Trapp identifies three modes of argumentation: descriptive, relational, and evaluative.[6] Descriptive argumentation focuses on disputes about the nature and definition of things; relational argumentation concerns disputes about the relationship between things; and evaluative argumentation deals with disputes about the worth or value of things.

These modes of argumentation may operate independently of one another or they may be interconnected. A debate may, for example, revolve around that proposition that "violent video games should be banned." Because it considers the desirability of a ban on violent video games, this debate requires an evaluative mode of argumentation (e.g., "Is a ban on violent video games good or bad?"). Debaters quickly find, though, that in order to evaluate the desirability of this ban, they also must make arguments about whether video games depict realistic violence (descriptive argumentation) and whether the exposure to violence in the media causes the viewer to behave violently (relational argumentation). In this debate, all three modes of argumentation will be used. Given that most arguments in a debate serve one of these three modes of argumentation, you need to understand how to make arguments in each mode.

DESCRIPTIVE ARGUMENTATION

The descriptive mode of argumentation concerns the nature and definition of things. Descriptive argumentation occurs when people disagree about what something is. For example, when debating about the legalization of euthanasia, the parties involved often exchange descriptive arguments about whether euthanasia is murder. The participants arguing about this question would be engaged in the descriptive mode of argumentation. One side may claim that euthanasia, like murder, is a willful termination of human life. That arguer may claim that both involve an intentional act that results in the end of another's life, and therefore, euthanasia is equivalent to murder.

The opposing side may respond that while the similarity between murder and euthanasia described is accurate, murder — unlike euthanasia — occurs without the consent of the person whose life is terminated, and therefore, euthanasia is not like murder. Debaters exchange arguments like these, and others about the descriptions of euthanasia and murder, in an effort to establish the nature and definition of euthanasia. These arguers are engaged in descriptive argumentation.

Creating Descriptive Arguments

Arguers may create effective descriptive arguments in a variety of ways. Arguers may use the tactic of **differentiation** to demonstrate the nature of a thing. To do so, the arguer would place the thing under consideration into a general class and then differentiate that thing from the rest of the class. If arguing about the nature of global warming, a debater may claim that global warming is an increase of temperature on the earth's surface (class) caused by the atmospheric greenhouse effect (differentiation).

The use of **example** to describe the features of a tangible instance of the thing under consideration may help to illustrate that thing's nature and definition. Were I to argue that free trade allows Nike to export jobs to developing nations that do not have strong regulations to protect labor or the environment, I would be using an example of free trade to illustrate the nature and definition of free trade.

When comparing the thing under consideration to other, similar things, arguers may use **analogies** to demonstrate the nature and definition of that thing. To argue that the recreational use of marijuana should be legalized, debaters may compare how marijuana would be handled to the way in which alcohol is regulated. By drawing parallels between the management of these two intoxicants, the arguers hope to demonstrate the nature and definition of legalized marijuana.

Finally, arguers may rely on **authority** to establish the nature and definition of a thing. In so doing, the arguers are relying on someone or something with perceived expertise to define the characteristics of the thing in question. When presenting arguments about the nature of education, a debater may claim that education is a fundamental human right because it is identified as such in the Universal Declaration of Human Rights.

Opposing Descriptive Arguments

To counter arguments in descriptive argumentation, you will find several tests useful. First, you may test arguments by determining how **intrinsic** the characteristics associated with the thing being described are. Characteristics that are intrinsic to the thing being described are material to the description of that thing. On the other hand, those characteristics that are not intrinsic may be said to be immaterial to the description of the thing.

For example, when countering an argument that claims that capital punishment as practiced in the United States is racist, an opponent may claim that the characteristic of racism is not intrinsic to the act of capital punishment. He may assert that while the punishment may be administered in a way that is racially biased, the racially biased application of capital punishment is not an intrinsic characteristic of capital punishment. By doing so, he hopes to convince an audience that capital punishment may be practiced in a way that is not racially biased.

Another effective test of descriptive arguments is **thoroughness**. The test of thoroughness asks whether all the relevant characteristics of the thing being described have been identified. If the description is not sufficiently complete, the description is not adequate. If, for example, a debater were arguing on behalf of laws to prohibit the use of drugs, she might claim that such laws seek to protect people from activities that may be harmful. An opponent of such laws could counter by saying that such laws not only protect people from themselves but also represent, for some of the law's advocates, the expression of a moral opposition to recreational drug use. As such, a characterization of the laws as exclusively benevolent is not a sufficiently thorough description of antidrug laws.

RELATIONAL ARGUMENTATION

In the relational mode of argumentation, debaters exchange arguments about the relationship that exists between things, usually causal relationships.[7] Argumentation about causal relationships is concerned with the ability and likelihood of one phenomenon or event producing another. Whether making drug use illegal decreases the consumption of those drugs; whether capital punishment deters crime; and whether violence in the media causes actual violence are all subjects of relational argumentation about causal relationships.

Causal argumentation concerns relationships about which we can never be certain. We know, for example, that rain is caused by humidity in the air and a catalyst around which that humidity can condense until it gains the weight necessary to fall to the ground. We can verify the causal relationship between humidity, dust, and rain in both natural and contrived settings. In essence, the cause of rain falling is no longer a subject of argumentation; it is accepted as fact. Unfortunately, we don't have this level of confirmation for many other relationships.

For example, we don't know exactly what will happen to global weather patterns should the mean temperature of the earth continue to rise. In fact, we won't know for certain what the effects of climate change will be on weather until after it has occurred. We can, however, make causal predications about what we believe will happen based on the information we have. In other words, we engage in relational argumentation about what we cannot (or cannot yet) know. This is particularly relevant in debating: it is these unresolved (and as yet unresolvable) relational questions that prompt debates in the first place. Consider any debate about human behavior: human motivation—the focus of a significant portion of causal argumentation in debating—is rarely explained to an indisputable degree. When we propose laws or regulations that seek to constrain certain behaviors, we do so because we hope that such regulations will affect human behavior; that hope is based on causal reasoning that, at best, produces enough certainty to allow us to act. We cannot say with absolute certainty what the causal effect of the regulation will be, but we're led to believe—through causal reasoning—that the outcome will be that which we desire.

For those relationships that are unverified or unverifiable, we need to make arguments on behalf of (or in opposition to) the alleged relationships between phenomena. There are several ways to make effective arguments about causal relationships.

Creating Relational Arguments

One of the most effective ways to make broad, comprehensive causal arguments about relationships is to employ the technique of **reduction**.

Reduction proposes that a general claim about a causal relationship (i.e., one difficult to predict) will be reflected in a more narrow consideration of that same causal relationship (which is easier to predict). If, for example, I wanted to argue that harsher penalties for driving while intoxicated would decrease drunk driving, I might reduce the asserted causal relationship to an examination of one person's behavior: I may argue that *I* would be less likely to drive drunk if *I* knew that my first conviction would result in significant jail time; therefore we should pass harsher sentences.

You can employ reduction in several ways. First, an arguer may reduce the asserted causal relationship from a generalization about a class to one member of that class. The argument about the effect of harsher punishments for drunk driving is an example of this approach.

Another approach to reduction is to substantiate arguments about broad causal relationships within a class by narrowing the consideration to the characteristics of that class. If I argue that we can motivate consumers to use renewable energy by offering subsidies that would make it cheaper than non-renewable sources, I may substantiate that claim by pointing out that people (consumers) are self-interested and greedy and will therefore seek products that are cheaper.

Another way to make causal arguments is through the use of **analogies**. This strategy asserts a causal relationship between things by comparing the unknown instance with circumstances that are known. If I argued that creating a public health system would solve the health care crisis in the United States and I offered as support the effectiveness of public health care systems in Canada and the United Kingdom, I would be using analogies to establish the projected causal relationship.

A final way to establish causal arguments is to rely on **authority**. By referring to an expert whose credentials make credible her assertions about the nature of the causal relationship, a debater may establish the likelihood of the asserted causal relationship. If I create an argument that global climate change is the result of increased levels of greenhouse gases in the atmosphere, I may turn to the opinion of scientists who have studied the issue to substantiate my claim.[8]

Opposing Relational Arguments

Because reasoning about causal relationships is so fundamental to our understanding of the world around us, it is no surprise that there are a number of ways to test the validity of these arguments. These tests, applied to an opponent's causal argument, are a compelling way to counter them.

A very basic test of causal arguments is the test of **capability**. Before inquiring about the likelihood of the causal relationship asserted in an argument, this test asks whether the alleged cause is capable of producing the alleged effect. Those who contest the deterrent effect of capital punishment often use this test to undermine the causal relationship asserted by those who claim that capital punishment will deter murder. Most murder, opponents claim, is an act of passion, not the product of rational contemplation. Accordingly, a deterrent that requires the potential criminal to ponder the consequences of his behavior will fail. In other words, capital punishment will not deter murder.

A second test of causal reasoning is the examination of whether the causes are **necessary and sufficient** to produce the alleged effect. *Necessary* causes are those required to bring about an alleged effect: the presence of oxygen is a necessary cause of combustion. *Sufficient* causes are those that will, by themselves, bring about the alleged effect. While oxygen is required for combustion, it will not, by itself, produce combustion. An argument asserting a causal relationship may be compromised by demonstrating that the cause is either not necessary (and therefore the relationship isn't certain) or is not sufficient (and cannot, therefore, be isolated as a cause of the alleged effect).

The **absence** test is another way to assess causal relationships. To employ the absence test, an arguer would prove that without the alleged cause, the effect continues to exist. This observation makes the alleged causal relationship suspect. When countering an argument that violence in the media produces actual violence, I may claim that violence has been a part of human behavior since the dawn of time and, therefore, violence cannot be blamed on the media. In other words, absent the alleged cause (violent media) the effect (violence) still exists.

Correlativity is another significant factor in establishing compelling causal arguments. This test assesses the co-occurrence of the alleged cause and effect. Underlying the test of correlativity is the assumption that if the cause and effect are indeed related, as the cause increases (or decreases) the effect will simultaneously increase (or decrease). When attempting to establish the connection between antioxidants and the absence of cancer, researchers supported their claim of a causal connection by examining the rates of cancer in those cultures whose diets included a large amount of foods rich in antioxidants. By demonstrating that as one condition (antioxidant consumption) increased, the other (cancer rates) decreased, the researchers were able to make a compelling argument for a causal connection between the two.

Another common test of alleged causal relationships is the test of **alternativity**. Alternativity asks whether there are other causes capable of producing the same effect. If so, the causal relationship the debater asserted is suspect. The debate about global climate change at one point focused on the test of alternativity to determine whether an increase in greenhouse gases was to blame for global warming. Those opposed to the greenhouse gas explanation attempted to argue that the earth experiences natural cycles of warming and cooling that change the global climate; their point was to demonstrate that since an alternate cause (a warming cycle) was capable of producing the same effect (global climate change), the alleged cause (greenhouse gasses) was suspect.

The relational mode of argumentation establishes and tests alleged relationships between phenomena. By themselves, though, relational arguments are seldom sufficient. Typically, relational (and descriptive, for that matter) argumentation is developed in service, ultimately, of evaluative argumentation.

EVALUATIVE ARGUMENTATION

Through evaluative argumentation we determine what is good and bad, desirable or undesirable, favorable or unfavorable. Motions such as "This house fears the rise of China" or "This house would ban violent video games" are typical examples of motions that ultimately demand an evaluative mode of argumentation. The vast majority of argumentation that occurs in competitive debating culminates in evaluative argumentation.

Creating Evaluative Arguments

Creating evaluative arguments requires two steps: identification of the components of evaluation and comparison of those components.

The identification step makes explicit the components inherent in evaluative arguments: the *object* (or objects) being evaluated and the *evaluator*. The object is the focus of the evaluative effort: in the motion "This house fears the rise of China," the object being evaluated is "the rise of China." The evaluator is the term or phrase that implies a value judgment: in the example motion, "fears" is the evaluator.

Before that proposition may be tested, however, the object and evaluator must be defined. As noted earlier, this is where the descriptive mode of argumentation plays a role. To describe "the rise of China," teams may refer to China's increasing economic influence, its increasing political clout around the world, or its rapidly rising military. Of course, teams also may argue that all three of these factors or some other factor best defines China's rise.

The evaluator also requires definition. To prove that something is good or bad requires the arguer to define what constitutes "good" or "bad." In our example, before an adjudicator will be convinced that China's rise should be feared, she needs to know what constitutes "fear-worthiness." The definition of the evaluator produces a standard for evaluation. If I were to argue that a significant consolidation of power in one nation, unchecked by a relatively equal accumulation of power in another, competitor nation is a circumstance to be feared, I would have defined the evaluator in our motion. That definition, then, becomes the standard against which China's rise may be evaluated.

Ideally, the definition of the evaluator and the resulting standard should be phrased universally, applicable to all instances in which we evaluate like objects. Such universalized standards are most easily thought of as conditional statements about the class of objects under consideration. Typically, such standards are phrased as follows:

"If an (object class) is (definition of evaluator), then it is (evaluator)."

In our example, the general class to which China belongs is "nations." Thus, our standard may read as follows:

"If a (<u>nation</u>) (<u>consolidates power unchecked by competing nations</u>), then that nation is to be (<u>feared</u>)."

This phrasing insures that the standard by which we evaluate the rise of China is also applicable to the evaluation of the rise of other nations. The universality of the standard increases the chances that the standard is a legitimate, objective tool for assessment rather than a benchmark created solely for the convenience of those seeking to prove a particular proposition.

The second step in evaluative argumentation is to compare the object to the standard. This is the more familiar step in the evaluative process; debaters naturally engage in this step when they formulate arguments about the value of things. In strict argumentative terms, the comparison of the object to the standard requires that those who seek to prove a certain evaluation of an object demonstrate that the object meets the standard. In our example, when the arguer offers proof that China's economic, political, and military rise represents the consolidation of unrivaled and unchecked power in that single nation, she is comparing the object to the standard.

Cases created to prove evaluative propositions may take two general forms: the case may be built around a single standard (such as the example above, where the single "unchecked accumulation of power" standard is used to evaluate China's economic, political, and military might), or cases may be built around several standards, each of which serves as proof of the evaluation. A case for the motion "This house would legalize euthanasia" may be built around three independent arguments: (1) that allowing euthanasia ends the suffering of the terminally ill; (2) that allowing euthanasia honors the individual's autonomy in making his or her own decision; and (3) that legalized euthanasia will avoid the considerable expense of caring for a terminally ill patient. In this case, each of those arguments contains an implicit and distinct standard by which to determine the desirability of legalizing euthanasia:

1. If a medical policy minimizes a patient's suffering, it should be legalized;
2. If a medical policy honors an individual's autonomy, it should be legalized; and
3. If a medical policy minimizes the financial burden of caring for a terminally ill patient, it should be legalized.

Finally, evaluative argumentation may consider two types of assessment: simple evaluative argumentation considers the evaluation of a single object against some standard. "This house fears the rise of China" considers only whether the development of China is something to dread. Comparative evaluative argumentation considers the relative evaluation of two or more objects: "This house prefers market solutions to government intervention in economic crises" asks the arguers to evaluate the relative worth of the market solutions and government intervention, not to prove that either is good or bad.

Opposing Evaluative Arguments

Arguments exchanged in the evaluative mode of argumentation are, like any other arguments, subject to the critique of an opponent. The opposition of evaluative arguments is built on three general approaches: arguers may challenge the definition of the object under consideration; they may challenge the standard used to evaluate that object; or they may challenge the measurement of the object against the standard.

Challenging the definition of the object occurs when an arguer believes that those proposing an evaluative argument have defined the object under consideration inappropriately or incompletely. An opponent may claim, for example, that evaluating China's rise by focusing on its economic, political, and military strength inappropriately skews the consideration of China's ascent. Also part of China's rise, the opponent may argue, has been the improved standard of living for many of its citizens, access to previously unavailable economic opportunities, and a loosening of restraint on dissent. If "China's rise" were to include these things, an opponent may argue, we may not be so compelled to fear it. Remember that descriptive argumentation concerns argument over how things are defined; all those techniques effective at proving an alternate definition will be relevant to this effort.

To *challenge the standard used to evaluate the object*, arguers should focus on proving that the standard their opponents offer is biased or incomplete. In our previous example, the standard of "unchecked accumulation of power" was proposed as a standard by which we could determine whether to fear a nation. To oppose those who seek to prove we should fear China, the opposition may claim that the standard is incomplete. The opposition may claim that by itself the accumulation of power is innocuous; only when that power is exercised belligerently should we fear a nation. By changing the standard by which "fearworthiness" is evaluated, the opposition hopes to convince the adjudicator that because China hasn't acted belligerently, it is not to be feared.

Finally, arguers may *challenge the measurement of the object against the standard*. In this approach, opponents typically accept the standard offered by those attempting to prove the evaluation but challenge the proof offered to measure the object against that standard. When an arguer asserts that China has amassed unchecked and unrivaled economic, political, and military power, an opponent may counter by demonstrating that China's interconnectedness with the global economy provides a significant check on its economic influence; that its political authority is tempered by other—particularly Western—nations that have equal or greater political power; and that China's military might is still insignificant relative to that of Russia and the United States, both of which serve as a balance to any military influence China might enjoy. By contesting the measurement of the object against the standard, the opposition creates doubt about whether we should fear China.

Understanding how arguments function and how they may be structured is a necessary precursor to understanding how those arguments may be exchanged in descriptive, relational, and evaluative modes of argumentation. With the techniques of developing and critiquing each of these types of argument firmly in hand, we may now begin to consider how to apply these techniques to your advantage in competitive debating.

CHAPTER 3

Stasis and Structure

One of the ongoing challenges debaters face when working in the medium of verbal arguments is making clear the relationship between the ideas they're trying to convey. Because the activity of debating requires immediate verbal exchange, the ideas with which the debaters work are transient, fluid, and constantly in motion.

Overcoming this challenge requires that you're able to identify those places where and times when arguments pause, if only momentarily, and thus may be more easily recognized and manipulated. Known as points of stasis, these places represent the cornerstones of foundations on which more complex structures of argument may be constructed.

To understand the nature and function of points of stasis, we'll first examine a popular metaphor for argument that imagines the process of argument as one marked by movement. From there, we'll come to understand how points of stasis function as places of rest for those moving arguments and how debaters can use those points to design and implement their strategies. Finally, we'll address how debaters can create arguments that effectively communicate both their substance and form to the other participants in the round.

Argument as Movement

In their influential work *Metaphors We Live By,* George Lakoff and Mark Johnson discuss the role that metaphors play in our understanding of the world.[9] In general, they contend that humans come to understand the world around them by exchanging information in the form of metaphors that provide a familiar context in which to comprehend new information. Because these metaphors inherently express our version of reality, Lakoff and Johnson believe that the study of these metaphors can illuminate our understanding of the world. I believe this same illumination may be achieved by examining a metaphor prevalent in our discussions of argumentation.

One of the most frequently used metaphors for argumentation is that of movement. Consider the descriptions of what people do when they argue. Those who argue:

> *move* an audience,
> *advance* positions,
> *sway* opponents,
> *redirect* questioning,
> *follow* lines of argument,
> *take* logical leaps,
> *retreat* from claims,
> *push* issues,
> *drive* points home,
> *come* to conclusions,

and so on. This metaphor of movement is revealing of our perspective on argument.

When we talk about arguing using the language of movement, we imply at least two important things: first, we think of argumentation as dynamic, fluid, and transient; and second, we imagine argumentation having a spatial dimension. Understanding this metaphor more thoroughly provides the chance to overcome the challenge of a moving medium by finding ways to make that medium more stable.

To say that argument is dynamic, fluid, and transient builds on the model of argument discussed in Chapter 2. When examining the structure of arguments, we identified the basic model as one that represents the movement of an audience from that which they already believe (the support) to that which they don't yet believe (the claim).

The singular movement represented in this basic model of argument is repeated and amplified in the process of argumentation. Given that any particular position advanced by an advocate is a collection of simple arguments working in concert to prove a proposition, and given that an advocate makes her arguments in a context in which an opponent seeks to meet her arguments with his own arguments, and given that these opposing advocates work with partners in teams to advance their positions, and given that in Worlds-style debating there are four teams in each round, the complexity of potential movement in a round of debate is exponential. With so many simultaneous, competing efforts to move an audience, confusion is more likely than not.

But the metaphor of movement also offers the opportunity to overcome this confusion. The metaphor of movement implies that we conceive of arguments as existing in a spatial context; to move, something must exist in space (or at least be thought of as similar to something that exists in space). Though the arguments that are exchanged in a debate round don't have physical form, when we work with them — that is, when we construct our own arguments, deconstruct those of our opponents, or attempt to compare positions of the two sides — we do so by first affixing those arguments to a point of reference. This point —

this imaginary static place in the imaginary space in which arguments move—allows us to identify, understand, and evaluate competing arguments more effectively than we could if they remained in motion.

Points of Stasis

These fixed points are known as points of stasis. Stasis, first discussed by the ancient Greek and Roman rhetoricians, refers to an imagined place where competing arguments meet. If you and I disagree about where to get lunch—I want Indian food and you want Thai—the point of stasis for our disagreement concerns where we'll eat. In a debate, points of stasis are those places where the arguments we make meet the arguments our opponents make. If I argue that India should be granted a permanent seat on the United Nations Security Council (UNSC) and you argue that it should not, the *point of stasis* for our argument is whether India should join the UNSC. Two general points of stasis are relevant to debating: points of stasis that function as **propositions** and points of stasis that are **issues**.

PROPOSITIONS

In a debate round, a proposition is the most general point of stasis over which the opposing sides will disagree. A proposition serves two functions: first, the proposition serves as a boundary around the subjects being debated, and second, the proposition divides ground between those arguing for the proposition and those arguing against it.

The first function of a proposition is to identify those matters that will be the subject of argumentation in the debate and, perhaps more importantly, those that won't. A debate with the proposition "we should legalize euthanasia for terminally ill patients" may feature arguments about what euthanasia is, how doctors would react to legalizing euthanasia, and whether legalizing euthanasia is desirable. Debate about this proposition would not, however, feature arguments about the recreational use of marijuana; such arguments would be excluded by the proposition.

To continue the metaphor of movement and space discussed above, imagine that the proposition for debate acts as a boundary around the "field of play" for the debate round; it indicates what territory will be contested and what won't. Those arguments that occupy territory within the bounds of the proposition are relevant to the debate; those arguments in the territory outside those bounds are irrelevant.

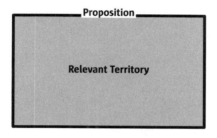

The proposition also functions as a dividing line between the territory that belongs to those arguing in favor of the proposition and those arguing against it. In the example of India's membership in the Security Council, the Proposition would make arguments for India's inclusion and the Opposition would make arguments against it; the division of this ground is represented by the proposition.

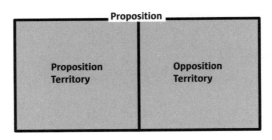

Frequently, the motion provided for the debate will express the proposition. For example, if the motion announced is "This House would criminalize the payment of ransom," the proposition for the debate is clear: the Proposition side will advocate for making payment of ransom illegal and the Opposition will argue that it should not be. The participants in the debate round (including the debaters, the adjudicators, and the audience) may anticipate that the Proposition side will advance arguments proposing penalties for payment of ransom and that the Opposition side will advocate that criminalization is an inappropriate way to discourage payment of ransom.

At other times, however, the proposition will differ from the motion assigned for the debate. It may do so for two reasons: first, the case presented by the Proposition side may be explicitly different from the motion; or second, the proposition may emerge organically as the product of the arguments and strategy pursued by the Proposition and Opposition teams.

In the first case, an Opening Proposition's case may become the proposition for the debate simply because some motions do not make good propositions. Vague, abstract, "fuzzy" motions do not clearly define the field of argument to be contested, nor do such motions clearly divide the ground between the Proposition and the Opposition. Consider a debate over the motion "This house would designate one city to permanently host the Olympic Games." Though such a debate may focus on the abstract benefits and costs of a single-city site for the Olympics, the debate would seem incomplete without identification of a particular city. In an effort to make the debate more concrete, the Opening Proposition team may, for example, identify Athens as the proposed permanent site for the Olympic Games. The *proposition* for the debate, then, becomes whether Athens should be designated as the permanent host of the Olympics.

The proposition in a particular round may also be the product of the team's implicit struggle over the appropriate focus for the debate. Consider the example of a motion such as "This House would require patients under 18 years of age to obtain parental consent prior to receiving an abortion." Given this motion, the general location of disagreement between the Proposition and Opposition sides could turn on whether legal abortion is a desirable or undesirable social policy; it could focus on whether young people under the age of 18 have the rational capacity to make a sound choice in these circumstances; or it could focus on whether or not parents are the best choice of adult to oversee such a decision. Ultimately, whichever of these questions the debate ultimately focuses on would be the proposition for the round.

ISSUES

In addition to the general point of stasis that defines the bounds and division of ground in the debate, other, more specific points of stasis — known as *issues* — are the meeting points of the particular arguments that are explored to answer the larger question (the proposition). Issues are similar to propositions, in that they represent the place where the arguments of the Proposition and the Opposition sides collide. They are different in scale and focus, however. Issues are more narrow points of stasis that emerge when the Proposition and Opposition make their arguments about the truth of the proposition. In other words, issues are the specific areas of clash within the field of consideration created by the proposition.

Imagined visually, issues relate to the proposition like this:

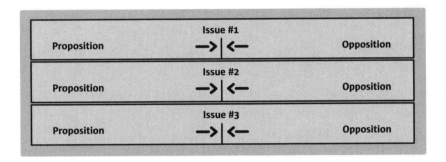

If, for example, the proposition for debate is "This house would ban smoking in public places," the Proposition and Opposition sides will likely disagree over specific areas of controversy within the greater proposition. These specific areas are the *issues* in the debate.

The two sides may disagree over the issue of public health, with the Proposition arguing that banning smoking in public will protect those who don't want to smoke from second-hand smoke and the Opposition arguing that little exposure to second-hand smoke occurs in public places. The Proposition and Opposition may clash over an economic issue, with the Opposition arguing that banning smoking in public places will affect profits both for retailers who will sell fewer cigarettes and the businesses that will lose revenue from smokers who will no longer patronize their now nonsmoking establishments. Finally, the two sides may exchange arguments about rights, with the Opposition arguing that smokers have a right to exercise their choices even in public places. The Proposition may respond that a smoker's right to indulge his choice is no longer guaranteed when that right negatively impacts a nonsmoker's right to avoid inhaling second-hand smoke.

Represented visually, the ban smoking debate might look like this:

This house would ban smoking in public places

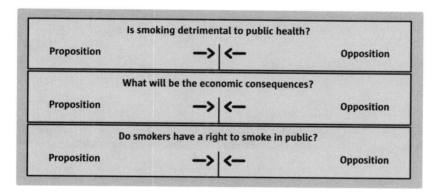

Issues are defined by the arguments debaters make to support their positions. If a debater argues that there will be some economic impact of a particular proposal, an economic issue exists in the round. If other debaters argue that a proposal affects the individual rights of the citizens, there exists a rights issue.

While these issues are initiated by the arguments made by the competing sides, they don't "mature" as issues unless they are engaged by the other side. If, in the smoking debate, the Proposition argues that smoking is detrimental to public health and the Opposition doesn't offer arguments to contest that claim, not much occurs within that issue. To say that the issue doesn't mature, however, is not to say that it isn't significant. Uncontested, the issue may go decisively to the Proposition. Alternately, the Opposition could ignore the substance of the issue but argue that it is insignificant when compared to other issues (which the Opposition would likely win). More on this later.

Though these issues are defined by the arguments debaters make, some of the issues are predictable, as they emerge time and again in debates, particularly in those debates over propositions of public policy. What follows is a list of issues that regularly emerge in competitive academic debates. Although this list is by no means exhaustive, it is a good reference for debaters who are seeking to anticipate what arguments may be made relative to any proposition.

Issue	Subject
Cultural	Arguments about the collective identity shared by people in a particular group.
Economic	Arguments concerning financial matters.
Educational	Arguments relevant to the effort to instruct citizens.
Environmental	Arguments about the natural world.
Legal	Arguments related to what is required or prohibited by a society's rules.

Moral	Arguments concerning ethical consequences of a proposition.
Political	Arguments relevant to the acquisition and exercise of power.
Rights	Arguments about freedoms or privileges.
Security	Arguments that address the subject of a nation's safety.
Social	Arguments regarding relationships between people.
Symbolic	Arguments concerning the interpreted meaning of phenomena.
Welfare	Arguments about public health and well-being.

Note that the scope of the above issues is not fixed. Take, for example, the "ban smoking" debate discussed above. Though the arguments regarding the economic consequences of a smoking ban may be gathered into a broad economic issue, that issue also could also be subdivided into more narrowly focused issues. Perhaps the Proposition and Opposition disagreed on the economic impact for commercial interests (such as cigarette retailers and bars and restaurants that may lose smokers' business) and for the public interest (such as the costs to public health systems from smokers). In this case, the general issue of "economic" arguments might better be divided into "commercial economic" and "public economic" issues.

The Relationship(s) between Issues

Often, the issues that are developed to interrogate a proposition are unrelated. The issues in the debate discussed above—a public health issue, an economic issue, and an individual rights issue—are not interconnected in any logical way. Certainly they all share an affiliation with the topic; they are substantively relevant to the proposition. The order and sequence in which they are encountered, however, is not determined by any logical relationship between those points.[10]

Other sets of issues, though, have logical relationships with each other that demand a particular organization of those issues. Consider the motion "This house would require prisons to facilitate their prisoners' right to procreation." For this motion, the issues likely to serve as the points of contention between the Proposition and Opposition include the following:

1. Does a "right" to procreation exist?
2. Do prisoners enjoy a right to procreation?
3. Are prisons obligated to facilitate a prisoner's right to procreation?

These issues are logically progressive. The question of whether or not a right exists must be addressed before the issue of whether prisoners enjoy those rights can be considered. Similarly, before the debaters can take up the question of the obligation of prisons to facilitate prisoners' rights to procreate, the question of whether or not prisoners even have a right to procreate must be argued. The outcomes of these issues are similarly logically progressive: if the Opposition convinces the adjudicators that the answer to the first issue is "no," the proposition has been demonstrated to be false (there is no reason for prison officials to facilitate a prisoner's right to procreate if that right doesn't exist) and there is no reason to progress to the second issue. Similarly, if the Opposition proves that while a general right to procreation may exist, prisoners lose this right upon incarceration, there is no reason for the adjudicators to consider the third issue.

In some cases, the relationships that exist between issues emerge organically from the particular focus of a proposition. The prisoners' right to procreation debate, for example, features a logically progressive set of issues that are unique to that debate. A debate about legalizing the recreational use of marijuana would not feature the same logically progressive set of issues. Uncovering these proposition-specific issues requires that the debaters analyze the proposition for relevant sets of issues and, more importantly, for the potential logical relationships that may exist between those issues.

One way to do this is to determine if some issues serve as logical foundations for other, subsequent issues (or, conversely, if some issues rest upon preceding foundational issues). For the marijuana debate, for example, you might anticipate that teams will disagree about whether there exists a right to autonomy that is violated by prohibitions on the recreational use of marijuana. That issue — "is an individual's right to autonomy violated by a prohibition on the use of marijuana?" — rests on a *foundational, preceding* issue: "do individuals have a right to autonomy?" In the other direction, an issue that is *subsequent* to the "is autonomy violated" issue might be something like "is the violation of autonomy significant enough to outweigh the potential harms that may be incurred by legalizing the recreational use of marijuana?" Consequently, the issues as they may be defined for the marijuana legalization debate would be ordered in the following, logically progressive way:

1. Do individuals have a right to autonomy?
2. Is an individual's right to autonomy violated by a prohibition on the recreational use of marijuana?
3. Is the violation of autonomy significant enough to outweigh the potential harms that may be incurred by legalizing the recreational use of marijuana?

In other cases, certain logically interrelated sets of issues arise whenever propositions of a certain type are debated. Debates over propositions of public policy, for example, feature certain "stock issues" that consistently arise in those debates. Public policy debates, regardless of whether the policy considered is the continuation of the USA PATRIOT Act or the legalization of euthanasia, clash over the broadly contested issues of whether a *problem* exists and whether a proposed *solution* will resolve that problem. These two broad issues—problem and solution—may be divided further into more narrowly focused issues. The *problem* issue concerns both the *significance* of the problem (is the problem significant enough to warrant attention?) and the *cause* of the problem (why does the problem exist?). Relevant to the *solution* issue is the more specific issue of the *solvency* of the solution (will the proposed solution solve or significantly reduce the problem?) and the *advantages and disadvantages* of enacting the solution (will the advantages of enacting the solution outweigh the disadvantages?).

Like the issues discussed above, the policy stock issues are related in a logically progressive way. Before considering whether a proposed policy would address the problem (the *solvency* of the proposed solution), the debaters must first address the question of whether the problem exists. Similarly, before considering the solvency of the proposed solution, the debaters must identify the reason the problem exists (the cause stock issue). This pattern of resolving one issue before moving on to the next is repeated with each of the policy stock issues: the debate cannot focus on the cause of the problem until the significance of the problem has been demonstrated; the question of solvency follows a conclusion on the cause of the problem, and so on.

Recognizing the relationships that exist between issues can be a significant asset to both Proposition and Opposition teams. For the Proposition, accurately analyzing the issues and predicting the logical progression of those issues promote more effective preparation by allowing the debaters to prepare arguments for the issues and to anticipate likely areas of attack by the Opposition. For the Opposition, the advantage of the logical relationship between issues is clear: if each issue serves as a foundation for the next, then an Opposition team may focus their argumentative effort on a particular stage of the logical progression in an attempt to "break the chain" of logic that leads to the overall conclusion.

Controlling Points of Stasis

As noted earlier, the focus of the debate — and therefore the points of stasis — is the product of choices the debaters make. The proposition for the debate is the result of an agreement (either tacit or explicit) between the teams to focus on certain ground and ignore other, potential ground. Moreover, the issues within that proposition arise from the arguments the debaters make: if an argument is not made to define an issue, then that issue doesn't exist in the round.

The manipulation of points of stasis is critical to winning debates. To appreciate the importance of controlling these points of stasis, we'll now consider how issues operate within the territory defined by the proposition. Understanding how issues operate, relate to each other, and relate to the proposition will enable you to control the substance and focus of the round.

As noted above, issues represent the struggle between Proposition and Opposition efforts to prove (or disprove) certain arguments relevant to the larger proposition. Each issue, regardless of its focus, represents an effort by the respective sides to define, capture, and defend ground in the minds of the adjudicators. Throughout the course of the debate, each side makes an effort to move the line that divides ground in the issue, with the goal of occupying the most space at the end of the round. Represented visually, a "map" of the effort might look like this:

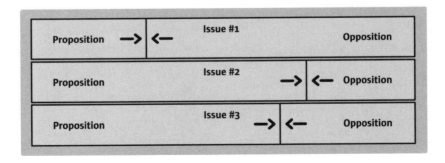

Based on this map, what happened in the round is clear: the Proposition won the debate because they held the majority of the ground. They prevailed on two of the three issues contested.

But to succeed, you must control not only the horizontal distribution of ground within each of those issues but the vertical expansion as well. This expansion, represented below, is the result of the debaters' efforts to demonstrate the relative importance of the issues they contest:

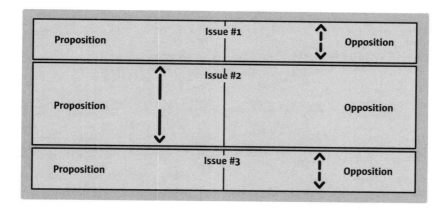

In this case, it's obvious that the most critical issue in the round was the second issue, which occupied the majority of the territory in the adjudicators' view. Winning this issue is critical to winning the round.

The second issue is the largest issue because the adjudicators believe it was the most important. Their estimation of the "critical" issues in the round may be the product of their own predispositions and preferences, but it is also subject to the debaters' efforts to convince them which issues are most important. Winning debaters don't risk letting the adjudicators decide which issues are most critical; their strategy of control requires that they not only prevail on the issues but that they prioritize the importance of those issues for the adjudicators.

I cannot overestimate the value of ranking the importance of issues. Debate is not merely a quantitative game of accumulating winning points; merely winning the most issues in the round does not guarantee that you'll win the debate. You must win the critical issues. Being able to correctly identify those critical issues and convince the adjudicators of the relative importance of those issues is essential to a winning strategy. It is this strategy that may allow you to lose a majority of the issues in a round but to prevail nonetheless. Consider the following map of the territory at the end of the ban smoking debate:

Proposition	Public Health?	Opposition
Proposition	Economic Consequences?	Opposition
Proposition	Smokers' Rights?	Opposition

In this debate, the Proposition lost the majority of issues; the Opposition prevailed on the economic consequences and smokers' rights issue; the Proposition won only the public health issue. Nonetheless, the Proposition convinced the adjudicators that the public health issue outweighed the other issues and, consequently, occupied the majority of territory at the end of the debate.

Structuring Arguments to Occupy Space

Just as a carpenter uses scaffolding to hold the pieces of a building together while it is being assembled, a debater needs scaffolding on which to fix the ideas that make up the argument she is constructing. Debaters work in the medium of oral communication; their speeches are constructed as they present them from only limited notes. Though they may have a rough outline of their ideas generated during their preparation, the speech exists only as potential until it is expressed. Imagine, then, this outline as the scaffolding to which the more complex and developed ideas in the speech will be affixed. Working from a few fixed points in a logical plan, the debater must "fill in the spaces" to create a coherent, fully developed expression of those ideas that conveys her complete strategy.

Unfortunately, the other teams in the round, your partner, and — most importantly — the adjudicators don't have a copy of your outline. Each of these participants will create their own record of the substance and order of arguments based on the cues you provide them in the debate. In addition to making your arguments, you must communicate the structure of the debate, clearly identifying the issues and how arguments interact within those issues (and how the issues interact with each other and, ultimately, the proposition).[11]

If we continue the metaphor of the debate as a territorial dispute between the Proposition and the Opposition, we can also imagine that we can map that territory to reflect the Proposition and Opposition's argumentative efforts as the debate progresses. To be able to establish, capture, and defend territory (that is, to communicate the structure of the round) requires that debaters communicate the structure of their arguments.

In the physical world territory is defined through boundaries. These boundaries are imaginary lines that represent a division of territory between individuals or groups. Although these boundaries sometimes follow geographical features (like rivers, coastlines, or mountain ranges), the boundary itself is entirely a human construct: there would be no line between China and Mongolia if the people of those two nations didn't recognize that boundary.

Similarly, the boundaries of territory in a debate are constructs. Rather than being surveyed and staked, though, these boundaries are established by the structure of the debaters' arguments. When we introduce an argument into the adjudicators' consideration, it begins to occupy space in their minds. When we address an opponent's argument, we contest the boundaries that define that argument, either by attempting to occupy more space than our opponents within an issue or by changing the adjudicators' perception of the relative importance of that issue. In all these efforts, we are communicating not only the substance of the argument but also its structure.

Just as physical boundaries are made obvious by physical indicators—such as fences, signs, and the like—the territory held by your arguments will be made clearer if you offer indicators of the structure of your arguments. In other words, all arguments that we make occupy space in the mind of the audience; the boundaries that define those arguments will be more evident to the other participants in the debate if we demarcate the boundaries with clear structure.

TAG LINES

To communicate the structure of your ideas, you must create effective **tag lines**. Tag lines are a one-sentence distillation of a complex argument intended to stick in the audience's mind (or in the audience's notes). Good tag lines have several common characteristics:

1. Tag lines should be *simple*: when writing a tag line, keep in mind that the audience won't recall (or write down) an entire complex argument verbatim. On the other hand, the participants may recall simple, elegant tag lines that capture the essence of the complex argument. Your tag lines should generally comprise a maximum of five to seven words.

2. Tag lines should *express a single idea*: a tag line should be sufficiently broad to capture a fully developed complex argument.

At the same time, it should be narrow enough that it expresses the thesis of that argument as a single thought. Effective tag lines are phrased to express a solitary memorable idea.

3. Tag lines should be *declarative*: they should express clearly a stance relative to the motion. Interrogative tag lines (those phrased as questions) have a place, particularly when the debater wants to give the impression of neutrality, but in general the tag line should state unambiguously the orientation of the argument.

4. Tag lines should be *phrased assertively*: while overstating a claim is a mistake, creating a kernel of an argument that doesn't capture the power of the argument is also an error. As the part of the argument that the other participants are likely to recall most readily, the tag line should effectively summarize the direction and force of the argument.

Using these guidelines, we can see that a tag line like

"Corporal punishment teaches children to be violent"

is superior to the following examples:

"By providing models of violence administered by authority figures they're likely to respect, corporal punishment teaches children to be violent."

"Corporal punishment teaches children to be violent and stunts their emotional development and maturity."

"Does corporal punishment teach children to be violent?"

"Corporal punishment may have a residual effect beyond the intended punitive message: children who encounter violent behavior may eventually display such behavior themselves."

Remember, a tag line is not an argument. If anything, the tag line most closely resembles the claim an argument seeks to advance (though tag lines may represent support or inferences too, depending on the circumstances). Regardless of what role it plays in the argument it represents, its function as a structural device is clear: a tag line is the placeholder for a more complex idea or set of ideas.

Consider our example: in a debate, the tag line "Corporal punishment teaches children to be violent" would represent a complete argument that would be substantiated by other ideas organized as support for the main claim. These supporting ideas too may be expressed in tag lines:

Corporal punishment teaches children to be violent
a. Children learn by modeling behavior
b. Violent incidents create particularly vivid models

Most often you will organize these tag lines into an outline that serves as the notes from which you will speak; similarly, those listening to your speech will typically record the main ideas expressed in the speech in outline format. You can think of this outline as the map of the speech: if designed well and followed closely, it may improve your chances of reaching your goal. Like a map, an outline is useful both prospectively—for you to plan and recall where you intend to go—and retrospectively—for the other participants to review after the speech and recall how they arrived (or how the speaker intended for them to arrive) at a particular goal. As such, the communication of structure is critical to a debater's strategy of control.

STRUCTURAL DEVICES

The easiest way for a debater to communicate this structure would be to provide each participant a written outline, but in most cases, she will not have that luxury. Instead, she will have to communicate the argument's structure in the same way she communicates its substance: in the speech itself. Fortunately, some simple **structural devices** may help to convey this structure. The most effective structural devices are often the most simple:

1. An effective speech should be built around an *introduction* that invites the audience to understand the rest of the speech; a *body* that conveys the substance of the message; and a *conclusion* that summarizes and provides a definite ending for the speech.

2. The introduction of the speech should contain a *preview* that forecasts the development of the main arguments in the body of the speech. The conclusion should feature a *review* of those same arguments.

3. Between each of the major arguments developed in the body of the speech, the speaker should offer clear *transitions* that tell the audience what has just been said and what will next be said. Transitions also help to illustrate the relationship between the arguments offered.

4. *Parallel structure* requires that the major arguments are presented in the same order each time they are discussed. Thus, if the

speaker previews three reasons why corporal punishment should be made illegal (it teaches violence, it stunts the emotional development of children, and it's tantamount to child abuse) in her introduction, she should discuss them in this order in the body of the speech and review them in the same order in the conclusion.

5. Intangible ideas become more fixed and substantive when they are referred to *redundantly* and *consistently*. Though the technique should not draw attention to itself, redundancy goes a long way toward cementing an idea in the mind of an audience, particularly if what's repeated is a well-phrased tag line that is presented in the same way every time the speaker refers to it.

If you use these techniques, you will increase the chances that your argument follows an evident structure. If the structure of an argument is evident, the other participants in the round will take note of the argument's clarity and progression. Such arguments occupy the most space in the minds of the other participants and, therefore, likely command the majority of attention in the debate. Well-structured arguments are critical to effective debating.

CHAPTER 4

Basic Strategy and Skills

Competitive academic debating is defined by your effort to prevail over the other debaters against whom you are competing. When you enter a debate competition, you are committing to the shared assumption that you will do your best to represent the position to which you've been assigned and to challenge the efforts of the other teams to do the same. In short, your primary objective is to win. Other goals often articulated as motivating forces for debaters—such as personal growth, education, pursuit of truth, etc.—are rooted in (and benefit from) the pursuit of victory.

You are most likely to achieve this overriding objective when the pursuit of the goal is guided by an overarching strategy. That strategy need not be complex but it should be acknowledged. But having a strategy is not enough; winning teams must develop and master the basic skills that allow them to pursue their strategy.

This chapter looks at a comprehensive strategy that serves well the goal of winning. Once I've explained the strategy, I'll turn my attention to the skills you need to implement it.

A Strategy of Control

Debate is a contest of control: those who win debates are typically those who are most adept at controlling what happens in the round. Some things—like what the other team says—are difficult to control.

Other things — such as which arguments and issues the adjudicators believe to be most important — are easier to control. In either case, though, the team who most effectively controls the round is most likely to win.

Perhaps one of the most elusive concepts for inexperienced debaters to grasp is this: what happens in a debate is not inevitable, accidental, or outside your control. What happens in a debate is the product of choices debaters make. Far too many debaters approach a debate round from a passive perspective, believing their responsibility is to merely track and respond to what happens in the round. As a consequence, these debaters are often insecure in their abilities: they seem to believe that others in the round (including the adjudicators) have an unequivocal understanding of the issues being debated and the way in which those issues should be debated. They struggle throughout the round to avoid mistakes that may reveal their ignorance to the other — presumably in-the-know — participants. They see their efforts as subject to the forces of the round beyond their control.

These debaters should instead focus on determining, designing, and directing what happens in the round. Recall the first chapter, in which I discussed a philosophy of debating that recognizes that meaning is not fixed and that argument is the medium through which we convince others to accept our interpretations of the world. This assumption is what led Foucault to believe that power was held by those who have control over what words mean. Debate is no different: those who control the discussion will likely control who wins the round.

A strategy of control seeks to put you in charge of what the round is about and what is relevant to the debate. Your strategy must seek to control the perceptions of the audience; winning debaters control not only *what* the participants in the round think about but also *how* those participants think about the substance of the round. Winning debaters see the round in its entirety, not merely as individual arguments; they understand how to integrate their arguments with those of the opposition and how to compare the positions taken by each side. They control the issues under consideration, the labels by which those issues are recognized, and the order in which those issues are discussed. Winning debaters are reluctant to leave to the adjudicator the decision of which arguments are better; they actively seek to critique and challenge the arguments of their opponents and to compare and contrast their opponents' arguments with their own. A debate will more likely be won by a team that provides the adjudicator with a structure and approach for comparing their arguments rather than a team that leaves that comparison entirely to him.

To exercise a strategy of control requires mastery of the concrete skills that allow debaters to take charge of a round. In general, you need to gain competency in three basic skills: constructive argumentation, deconstructive argumentation, and framing. Constructive argumentation and deconstructive argumentation are two sides of the same coin: constructive argumentation refers to building the arguments for your position; deconstructive argumentation is critiquing the other teams' efforts to do the same. Preceding and following constructive and deconstructive argumentation, framing is the effort that guides the adjudicators' (and, if done well, the other teams') perception of the predominant focus for the debate and of whose arguments best serve that focus.

Constructive Argumentation

The act of building arguments is fundamentally about giving ideas substance. To communicate something as intangible as an argument — a series of ideas related to each other in a particular, typically linear way — requires both that you fully understand the relationships between those ideas and that you express those relationships with such clarity that the interconnectedness of the ideas is clear.

Building successful arguments requires first that the debater discover the potential arguments for or against the proposition. Once a debater has collected a variety of potential arguments, he or she must think carefully about how those arguments will be assembled into a holistic effort to prove (or disprove) a proposition. Constructive argumentation refers both to the development of individual arguments and the coordination of those arguments into a coherent case; more broadly, these efforts are known as analysis and synthesis.

THE ANALYTIC PROCESS

Analysis is the process of taking ideas apart; for our purposes, the goal of this disassembly is to see more clearly the components of an argument. Analysis is a necessary starting point because the reasoning that underpins the conclusions we embrace isn't always clear, even to those who express those conclusions. Analysis allows us to dissect ideas to uncover the reasons that serve as foundation for those ideas.

Many arguments operate as enthymemes. An enthymeme is a type of argument that leaves some premise(s) or conclusion(s) unstated, trusting that the audience will fill in the missing parts. If I were to argue that parents should be prohibited from administering corporal punishment, I might say something like

"Corporal punishment is no different than child abuse"

trusting that my audience would fill in the missing parts of the argument:

(Child abuse is abhorrent and illegal)

"Corporal punishment is no different than child abuse"

(Corporal punishment is abhorrent and should be illegal)

Our thinking about arguments is often similarly enthymematic. Rather than organizing our thoughts in rational patterns that lead from premises to conclusions, we often hold a mix of opinions, feelings, intuitions, and unquestioned assumptions that operate as the basis for our thought. From this basis emerge the ideas we use to convince others. Obviously, if we better understand how our thoughts are (or may be) interconnected and organized, we'll be better able to convey that interconnection and organization to others.

Another reason to begin the constructive process with an analytic effort is to discover the potential bases of support for the conclusions we want to convey to our audience. As discussed in Chapter 2, the most basic function of argument is to connect that which an audience does not yet believe and accept (*claims*) to that which they already believe and accept (*support*). Analysis allows us to anticipate likely areas of support our audience may accept.

The analytic process is straightforward. It's focused around a single question that prompts inquiry: "why?" This simple question initiates the search for the reasons on which you will construct the arguments that support your case. You may pursue two directions of inquiry by asking "why?": analysis for *depth* ("drilling down" into arguments) and analysis for *breadth* ("thinking laterally" about reasons).

Analysis for *depth* seeks to find the ground on which claims rest. The first question you ask when assigned your position is "why?" If assigned to defend the motion "Corporal punishment of children should be made illegal,'' your initial inquiry might produce the answer "because corporal punishment is the same as child abuse." As you compile the answers to the initial "why?" question, you should interrogate each answer: asking "why?" again might lead a debater to index the ways in which corporal punishment and child abuse are similar: both involve dramatic power differentials between adult and child, both involve physical violence, both are often administered in an intense emotional state, etc. Continuing to ask "why?" for each subsequent answer prompts the debater to continue to dig into the reasons underpinning the claim until she discovers that which she believes will function as a base of support shared by the audience. In the terms used by the model of argument discussed in Chapter 2, you will know that you have "drilled down" far enough when you believe the audience will accept your support. This shared base then serves as the foundation on which to construct the argument.

Equally important is analysis for *breadth* of reasons. Thinking laterally about the support for a claim with the goal of generating diverse reasons for it can often produce novel and equally compelling areas of support. Rather than the simple "why?" question employed by the inquiry for depth, inquiry for breadth may be best thought of as asking "why else?" "Why else" should corporal punishment be made illegal? "Because corporal punishment is ineffective at changing children's behavior." "Because corporal punishment encourages children to use violence to respond to problems." You should subject these answers, and others discovered in the analytic process, to analysis for depth to ensure that you have discovered a foundation of thought the audience is likely to accept.

Of course, not all analysis using this method will be productive. With this method you cannot discover what you don't know; debaters often lack an answer to the "why?" or "why else?" questions. Continuing to inform yourself about options for argument is a given for any winning debater. But even when you previously have encountered material that would help you answer the "why?" or "why else?" questions, the answer (or at least the best answer) may not always be forthcoming. In such cases, you may benefit from a more structured approach to your analysis that provides insight into potential areas of argument.

When discussing the invention of arguments, rhetorical scholars from Aristotle to Perelman have cataloged "starting points" for the creation of arguments in an attempt to assist arguers with this generative process.[12] These starting points serve as prompts for remembering or discovering potential areas of support for the claims we hope to prove. In the previous chapter, we discussed a set of predictable issues that consistently arise in debates over public policy. These issues may serve as prompts for your analysis of potential arguments.

Issue	Subject
Cultural	Argwuments about the collective identity shared by people in a particular group.
Economic	Arguments concerning financial matters.
Educational	Arguments relevant to the effort to instruct citizens.
Environmental	Arguments about the natural world.
Legal	Arguments related to what is required or prohibited by a society's rules.

Moral	Arguments concerning ethical consequences of a proposition.
Political	Arguments relevant to the acquisition and exercise of power.
Rights	Arguments about freedoms or privileges.
Security	Arguments that address the subject of a nation's safety.
Social	Arguments regarding relationships between people.
Symbolic	Arguments concerning the interpreted meaning of phenomena.
Welfare	Arguments about the public health and happiness.

Additionally, there are well-worn sets of related concepts that also may serve as a prompt for discovering arguments. These sets are useful for both organizing your arguments about a particular position and discovering what those arguments are. For example, a debater who refers to the "past-present-future" concept set as a starting point of analysis for the corporal punishment motion may be inspired to build a case around three points: the historical role of corporal punishment, the ways in which our present perceptions of parenting have changed, and the future of our development as a civilization should we continue to sanction corporal punishment.

Concept Sets
Past — Present — Future
Idealism — Realism
Moral — Pragmatic
General Principle — Specific Instance
Social — Political — Economic
Diplomatic Influence — Economic Influence — Military Influence
Domestic — Foreign
National — Regional — Global
Problem — Cause — Solution
Cause — Effect
Behaviors — Motivation
Individual — Community
Empirical — Logical
Scientific — Spiritual

Regardless of the process used or the tools employed, the goal of the analytic process is to generate options from which to choose when developing coherent arguments for or against a proposition. But options are not coherent arguments; hence the need for synthesis.

THE PROCESS OF SYNTHESIS

Analysis is only the first of two steps in the constructive process: a well-built constructive effort is more than a mere a catalog of reasons for (or against) a proposition. Once you have options for arguments from which you may choose, you must then synthesize your arguments into a coherent plan to prove or disprove a proposition. Synthesis is the process of assembling the raw material generated by the analytic process into a compelling persuasive effort.

Synthesizing arguments into a coherent whole requires that the debater first consider the **logical progression** of those arguments.

As discussed in Chapter 2, arguments organize ideas to help audiences proceed from evidence to conclusions. In the narrowest sense, logical progression informs how arguments must be arranged; evidence should be presented as foundation from which audiences may proceed to obvious conclusions. More importantly, once the ideas within a particular argument are logically progressive, that argument must be arranged in a logically progressive organization with other arguments.

How should you decide which arguments go first? Which are second? And which arguments are subsequent to those? Fortunately, we already have some clues as to how to answer these questions: we know that arguments attempt to identify common bases of support shared by arguers and audiences. We know that support functions as the common starting point from which we proceed. Given that we may commonly share belief in certain bases of support, it should come as no surprise that arguers and audiences may also share the paths we travel to move from support to claim. If we structure our ideas in patterns familiar to our audiences, our audiences are more likely to understand (and be compelled by) our arguments. The organization of your arguments will benefit from understanding the patterns of thought common to human cognition and the logically progressive structures those patterns suggest.

In the early 20th century, Gestalt psychologists studied how we understand and integrate information. The product of their study was, in part, a number of perceptual principles that explain how we comprehend what we perceive. Taken broadly, these perceptual principles can be thought of as common patterns of thought.[13]

Three patterns of thought are most relevant to your effort to structure your arguments in a familiar, logically progressive way: closure, proximity, and similarity.

The pattern of **closure** suggests that human cognition abhors the incomplete. When we encounter information, we make sense of it in part by attempting to recognize the beginning and the end of the data. Information organized in a way that emphasizes the initiation of an idea and the eventual resolution of that idea will be compelling for an audience. Several logical progressions are suggested by this pattern of thought:

Problem/Solution: a logical progression common to many persuasive efforts, the problem/solution progression first establishes the significance of a problem and then advocates for a solution to that problem. By way of example, a case using this progression may be structured to first explain the number of Americans lacking health insurance and the consequences of that situation and then turn to how a system of universal health care would solve the problem.

Principle/Application: arguments using this progression should be ordered so that a general principle is first established as relevant. Following that, the principle may be applied to the concept being evaluated. A case that first argues that free speech is vital to democracy and then argues that hate speech is a valuable form of speech worthy of protection follows this logical progression.

Cause/Effect: as the name suggests, the cause/effect progression considers first the reasons for a phenomenon and then the attendant consequences of that phenomenon. For example, a debater may argue for radical redistribution of wealth by examining first the reasons why poverty exists and then turning her attention to the various consequences of being impoverished, thereby proving that redistribution of wealth is desirable because it would eliminate those consequences.

General/Specific: arguments may be ordered from the general to the specific, with the broadest arguments placed first and the subsequent arguments narrowing in scope. A case organized using this approach may open with general reasons why capital punishment doesn't deter crime and then turn its attention to a case study of a particular state where crime rates failed to drop after the adoption of capital punishment.

The pattern of **proximity** recognizes that humans may make sense of what they encounter by organizing information in ways that parallel how that information was encountered. Tying data to its origin in our experience provides context and continuity for the new information we encounter by connecting the information to that with which we're already familiar. Two logical progressions depend on the pattern of proximity.

Chronological: a chronological progression arranges information according to how it occurs in time. A case that argues for multilateralism in foreign policy actions may be structured chronologically by first examining the history of unilateralism as the chief mode of engagement in foreign policy, then by showing how the present circumstances have called that approach into question, and finally by demonstrating that the most pressing future international crises will require multilateral efforts.

Spatial: the spatial progression organizes information according to how it is exists in physical space. By capitalizing on the analogy to the tangible, this progression presents information in a very concrete and familiar way. A case that argues against the withdrawal of troops in Iraq by developing the consequences of a withdrawal for security in Iraq, for regional stability, and finally for global defense attempts to capitalize on a spatial progression.

The pattern of **similarity** recognizes that we naturally organize information we encounter by grouping it together with other, like information. In general, the principle of similarity compels us to identify themes in the information we encounter and to collect that information in groups defined by those themes. While the structural suggestion that emerges from this pattern of thought doesn't mandate a logical progression *per se*, it does remind us that the groups into which information is gathered should be inclusive (they should include all information on a particular topic), distinct (that the information in one group is not also contained in another group), and equivalent (the groups should be similar in scope). A topical structure adheres to the principle of similarity.

> *Topical*: the topical structure attempts to separate information relevant to a particular topic into appropriate subtopics of information. In so doing, the sub topics provide insight into the component elements of the main topic. Debaters may find the topical points of stasis discussed above particularly relevant to this effort. A case that argues against opening the Arctic National Wildlife Refuge to oil exploration by developing the economic, the environmental, and the cultural reasons not to do so would be organized in a topical way.

While arranging arguments in a logical progression is the goal of the analytic and synthetic processes, those well-ordered arguments will miss the mark unless they are communicated in a way that makes the structure of the argument evident to the audience. As discussed near the end of Chapter 3 in the section "Structuring arguments to occupy space," your effort to communicate the structure of your arguments may be improved by paying attention to your arguments' tag lines and your use of structural devices in your speech.

Deconstructive Argumentation

Mastering constructive argumentation — while an absolutely necessary element of successful debating — is not, by itself, sufficient to ensure success. In fact, when asked to describe debate, the effort to construct arguments would not likely be the first thing most people would use to explain the process. Instead, most explanations of debating would focus on countering opposing arguments.

Deconstructive argumentation refers to the process of taking arguments apart. To continue the building metaphor used to describe constructive argumentation, imagine that the deconstructive argumentation process is akin to a (very rigorous) building inspection. The goal of a building inspection, particularly for a recently constructed building, is to ensure that the structure is built well. The inspection ensures that those who will eventually occupy the building are fully aware of any structural shortcomings, deficits, or defects in the building. In a debate, deconstructive argumentation critiques the substance and structure of the opposing arguments so that the audience and judge are aware of the arguments' weaknesses and shortcomings.

More to the point, deconstructive argumentation produces the counterpoint to the opposing side's constructive point; it serves as the challenging force that meets an opponent's argument at a point of stasis. It is in these clashes between constructive and deconstructive argumentation that debate exists.

To successfully deconstruct an opponent's argument, you should adopt a critical mind set: simply put, the critical mind set is predicated on the awareness that you do not need to deconstruct every argument an opponent makes. This principle, while deceptively simple, is often remarkably difficult for debaters to grasp. Too many debaters take a "shotgun" approach to deconstruction; they seem to believe that they must counter every argument their opponents make. But so many other options exist: they may ignore the argument (provided the argument isn't critical to their own effort), they may concede the argument (if doing so doesn't compromise their own arguments or unnecessarily empower their opponents), they may demonstrate that the foundation on which the argument is built is not solid, or they may try to diminish the importance of an argument to their opponent's strategy. Of course, any of these approaches may be combined with others and all may serve a larger deconstructive effort.

Successful debaters have a variety of tactics available for deconstructing arguments, but the most elemental approach to deconstruction remains the direct critique of opponents' arguments. Successful deconstructive argumentation has two components: the evaluation of your opponents' arguments according to accepted **standards of argument quality** and the successful **structuring** of the refutation.

STANDARDS OF ARGUMENT QUALITY

Robert Trapp offers an insightful discussion of standards for argument quality centered on expectations for the evidence offered, the warrants employed and the claims advanced in arguments.[14] The standards of *acceptability, relevance,* and *sufficiency* provide debaters with a structured approach to the deconstruction of their opponents' arguments.

Acceptability

The standard of acceptability speaks to the quality of evidence on which an argument is based. Recall from Chapter 2 that the function of evidence is to ground the argument in an idea in which the audience already believes; support is the foundation from which the audience may be moved to accept the claim.

Using this standard, you may deconstruct an opponent's argument by demonstrating that the support offered for a particular claim isn't acceptable or accepted. If you can prove that the adjudicator should not accept the support (or that acceptable support has not been offered), the argument fails.

Generally, you may take one of three deconstructive postures relative to the acceptability of support offered for an argument.

1. The grounding for the claim is not apparent. This approach asks whether the argument being deconstructed contains a cogent subargument that establishes support for the claim. By the chain form of argument discussed in Chapter 2, you will recognize that this deconstructive approach attempts to expose the lack of support for the claim or for deeper levels of claims that, themselves, have been used as support for subsequent claims. Take, for example, the argument below:

Corporal punishment
should be made illegal

Corporal punishment is
no different from child
abuse, which is almost
universally illegal

As an argument, this one has the necessary elements: the claim is based on support intended to serve as a foundation for the claim.

An astute opponent, however, will recognize that this argument is more extended than the version presented and that the best deconstructive opportunities lie not in opposing the claim head on (to attempt to argue that corporal punishment should not be illegal) or even questioning the evidence (that child abuse isn't illegal), but in exposing the weakness of the support on which the support *itself* is based.

Thus, the deconstructive effort attempting to reveal the lack of a cogent subargument would focus on a lower level of support for the argument:

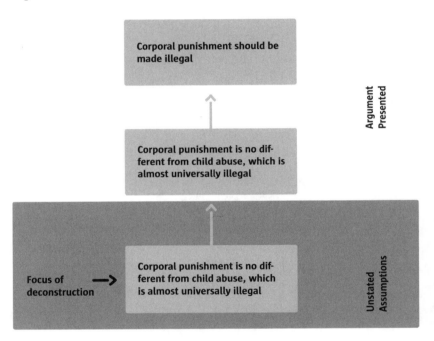

Here, the opponent would articulate the lack of similarities and the significant dissimilarities between corporal punishment and child abuse, thereby weakening the chain of reason that links support to claim.

2. The evidence offered is not generally known to be true. Arguments function by connecting the unknown (or the as yet unaccepted) to the known (or accepted). The second deconstructive approach aimed at acceptability is to challenge whether the support offered is generally known to be true. Imagine that an argument attempts to demonstrate that violence in the media leads to actual violence. The arguer may assert that people learn appropriate modes of behavior by either "practicing" their behavior in hypothetical situations or modeling the behavior of others, both of which are influenced by viewing violent media. It follows, asserts the debater, that if one is fed a steady diet of violent media, one is more likely to engage in actual violent behavior.

The opposition to this argument is clear: there exists no commonly accepted belief that people are incapable of distinguishing between actual violence and fictitious violence. In fact, common knowledge likely suggests exactly the opposite: most people have been exposed to violent images in popular culture but the vast majority of the population is not violent. The claim of a causal relationship between media and actual violence is compromised because of the support offered is not acceptable as common knowledge.

3. The evidence offered lacks external validation. Some support cannot exist in the realm of common knowledge, particularly opinion-based evidence or evidence that is the product of systematic collection, analysis, and reporting of data. For this type of support, a basis of credibility beyond that possessed by the debater making the argument is required. Deconstructing arguments by charging that the support offered lacks external validity may mean that an opponent attempts to undermine an argument by identifying the need for external validation of the support and the lack thereof, or by indicting the source of exter-nal validation (usually an "expert authority" or some publication).

If I attempt to argue that the risks of second hand smoke are overstated by relying on evidence produced by the Tobacco Institute, I would be open-ing myself to a critique by an opponent that my evidence lacks external validation. The Tobacco Institute, an organization founded and funded by tobacco producers with the express purpose of countering research that sought to demonstrate the health impacts of smoking, has been widely discredited. Any evidence produced by that source would be suspect.

Relevance

The second standard for testing the quality of an argument is rel-evance. Relevance addresses the inference for the argument; specifi-cally, the standard of relevance examines the quality of the connection between the support and the claim by asking whether the evidence offered is relevant to the claim made. If the support is relevant, the argument is likely to be of higher quality because an audience will be persuaded to accept the claim of the argument based on the support provided. An argument that relies on a relationship between support and claim that is demonstrated to be irrelevant is more likely to fail to convince an audience.

Standards of relevance are unique to the type of reasoning em-ployed by particular arguments. In fact, there are many different tests of relevance for each type of reasoning. While I won't catalog them all here, the table below provides a summary of the major test of relevance related to the most prominent forms of reasoning.[15] You may use each of the tests as a starting point for critiquing the relevance of support to claim for arguments you would like to deconstruct.

Argument by Example	Argument	"Our schools are no longer safe: look at what happened in Jonesboro, Arkansas; Littleton, Colorado; and Springfield, Oregon."
	Test	*Typicality*: are the examples typical?
	Response	"Though they happened around the same time, these incidents were anomalies. The vast majority of schools are peaceful and secure."
Argument by Analogy	Argument	"Alaska should legalize gambling; look at the amount of revenue generated in Nevada."
	Test	*Similarity*: are there adequate similarities between those things being compared?
	Response	"Alaska has neither the regulatory structure nor the tourist base of Nevada. There's no reason to expect that gambling would generate significant revenue."
Causal Argument	Argument	"The United States' effort to fight the Global War on Terror has actually produced greater numbers of terrorists."
	Test	*Alternativity*: Are there causes other than those asserted that might bring about the alleged effect?
	Response	"There are more terrorists now because of the rise of Islamic fundamentalism in these nations. Even without U.S. involvement, such fundamentalists would employ violence to affect change."

Argument from Principle	Argument	"Censorship, even of hate speech, is wrong because it is contrary to freedom of expression."
	Test	*Applicability*: Is the principle germane to the instance to which it is being applied?
	Response	"Free expression was intended to protect political speech. Punishing those who spew racial slurs does not affect a person's ability to engage in political valuable speech."
Argument from Authority	Argument	"Former U.S. surgeon general C. Everett Coop has made very clear that second-hand smoke is dangerous to nonsmokers' health."
	Test	*Credibility*: does the source making the statement have the qualifications to produce a credible claim on the subject?
	Response	"Dr. Coop's training and specialty was in pediatric surgery. He did little research on the consequences of second-hand smoke."

Argument by Incompatibility	Argument	"George W. Bush claims to want to make America more secure, yet his foreign policy inflames our enemies and alienates our allies."
	Test	*Inconsistency*: Do discrepancies of a degree sufficient to compromise the truth of either or both positions exist?
	Response	"Bush's foreign policy has had little real impact. Most of our important allies are with us in our effort to make the world secure, and those against whom we're fighting would be radical and violent with or without our foreign policy."
Argument by Dissociation	Argument	"I'm not opposed to government spending; I'm opposed to *wasteful* government spending."
	Test	*Legitimacy*: Is the division of the concept into dissociated categories a valid and comprehensive partition?
	Response	"There's a lot of gray area between good and bad spending. Many programs may have noble goals but are poorly managed. Reform, not elimination, is the answer."

Sufficiency

As a standard of argument quality, sufficiency asks whether the argument produces a level of certainty adequate for the audience to accept the claim. Diverse arguments, presented to varying audiences in distinct circumstances will require different levels of certainty in order to be accepted. Determining the level of certainty appropriate for any given argument is the concern of sufficiency.

Generally, the sufficiency required of any given argument is a function of the subject of that argument and the context in which it occurs.[16] The degree of proof necessary to make an argument compelling is tied to the subject of an argument: an argument to convince a local community assembly to install a traffic light at a busy intersection will require a different degree of proof than an argument to convince the UN Security Council to authorize the "preemptive" invasion of a country. The scope, magnitude, and consequences of each of these arguments differ dramatically; the degree of proof required for each should differ as well.

The context in which an argument occurs also influences the degree of proof an audience requires to accept an argument. Put simply, standards of sufficiency may vary given "where" the argument occurs.

Argument scholar Thomas Goodnight imagines that arguments function differently depending on where the argument is encountered. Goodnight describes the difference between the personal sphere of argument (that which exists between individuals who share an interpersonal relationship), the technical sphere of argument (that which exists between authorities in a particular field, such as medicine or engineering), and the public sphere of argument (that which exists between the members of a society related by the need to make collective decision).[17] One significant distinction between these spheres is that each requires a different force of effort to achieve a level of certainty sufficient for an audience to accept a claim in that particular sphere. In other words, the degree of proof required to convince an audience in the public sphere would likely be significantly different than that required to create a persuasive argument in the technical sphere.

Consider the debate over global climate change. To establish the impact of human activity on global climate change in the scientific (technical) sphere required years of data collection, analysis, and reporting, and testing various hypotheses. In the public sphere, much more informal efforts (such as the popularity of former vice president Al Gore's movie *An Inconvenient Truth*) constitute, for many, sufficient proof of the need to take action.

A useful approach to deconstructive argumentation may be found in the standard of sufficiency: to oppose an argument, you would contend that the argument does not meet a level of proof sufficient for the audience to accept it. You can accomplish this by examining the sphere of argumentation in which the argument exists ("My opponent's position may constitute sufficient proof for convincing a friend that a problem exists, but it doesn't establish the certainty necessary to serve as a basis for public policy") or by comparing the degree of certainty particular arguments achieve relevant to the consequence of each of those arguments ("We'll grant that we can't prove absolutely that withdrawing our troops from Iraq will produce a civil war, but the risks of doing so are so great that we should evaluate the argument in part on the mere risk of a negative consequence").

STRUCTURING REFUTATION

Like most other aspects of argument, your ability to structure refutation clearly is critical to your success. Developing the skills to structure refutation appropriately requires you to be aware of some general rules for structuring refutation and to master a specific pattern when deconstructing your opponents' arguments.

Generally, refutation will be more effective if it follows two rules. First, you should always refute an opponent's arguments before building (or rebuilding) your own. One simple maxim informs this rule: always leave the adjudicator on your own ground. When engaging in deconstruction, a debater is working on argumentative ground defined by her opponent.[18] That ground—no matter how well the debater refutes the arguments that define that ground—still belongs to your opponent. Even the act of refuting arguments on an opponent's ground has the effect of making those arguments more substantive to the judge. The principle of recency suggests that an audience is more likely to focus on and recall what they hear last: winning debaters always want to leave their audience thinking about their own arguments.

The other general rule is based on the assumption that even the simple act of identifying the arguments you intend to refute is part of the process of refutation. When you identify your opponents' arguments— the first step in effective refutation—you actually (re)present those arguments: you have the opportunity to cast those arguments in a way advantageous to you. Generally, the best approach to identifying arguments is to use the "one-off" approach, which takes what may be an opponent's complex, nuanced argument and reduces it to its essence. Thus, if your opponent has three major, fully developed, and supported lines of argument in his case, your refutation would begin by (re)presenting each as one single statement. In the end, then, you have reduced your opponent's seven-minute, well-developed case to three sentences, all of which receive adequate refutational attention from you (and all of which are dismissed in the first 1 minute 30 seconds of your speech).

A Structural Pattern for Refutation

While the effort to deconstruct an opponent's argument is complex, varied, and dependent on the substance of the argument and context in which those arguments are made, a standard approach to refutation can lend consistency and clarity to the effort. This pattern may be remembered by the acronym ICE: *Identify, Critique,* and *Explain.*

1. *Identify* the opponent's argument. The first step in effective refutation is to let the audience know which of your opponent's arguments you'll deconstruct. When possible, you should use the terms your opponent used to identify the argument. Of course, using your opponent's terms should be balanced with your effort to (re)present the argument in terms favorable to your side. In either case, your objective is to lead the audience to the argumentative ground on which your deconstruction will take place; if the adjudicator doesn't know to which of your opponent's arguments your refutation applies, your refutation will not likely be effective.

2. *Critique* your opponent's argument. This step is the most important in deconstruction: in this step you must identify the shortcomings of your opponents' arguments. You'll most likely accomplish this by referring to the standards of argument quality discussed above. You may critique your opponents' argument by claiming that the proof offered is not *acceptable* as evidence for the claim; that the proof offered is not *relevant* to the claim advanced; or that the argument does not develop a level of certainty *sufficient* to be accepted in this context.

3. *Explain* the significance of your deconstructive effort. The final step in the process of deconstruction is to explain the significance of your refutation. Here you tell the adjudicator why it matters that your opponent's argument fails in acceptability, relevance, or sufficiency. Most often this entails a discussion of the role the argument played in your opponents' broader case and why the absence of this particular argument weakens or negates that case. At this stage you may also compare your argument with your opponents' in a way that shows that your argument is superior.

Using the ICE approach, the deconstruction of an argument might proceed like this:

> In the first of their three arguments for making corporal punishment illegal, our opponents claim that corporal punishment is comparable to child abuse. [*Identification* of opponents' argument] This comparison is flawed: not only is corporal punishment long established as an acceptable mode of correction for children, it is motivated by love for the child and a desire to help the child learn right from wrong [*critique* of the opposing argument; application of relevance standard to show the analogy is flawed]. Because corporal punishment cannot be compared to the illegal act of child abuse, there exists no legal basis on which to prohibit corporal punishment and, consequently, no warrant for making corporal punishment illegal [*explanation* of the significance of the deconstruction].

Deconstructive argumentation is the engine of debating: testing competing arguments against each other distinguishes competitive debating from simple oratory. When grounded in the application of standards of quality for arguments and structured to promote the efficacy of the refutation, deconstructive argumentation will expose the weaknesses of opposing arguments and serve as a necessary step in persuading an audience to accept your arguments.

Framing

Building and critiquing arguments are important skills that successful debaters must master, but by themselves they are incomplete. In addition to constructing and deconstructing the arguments in the round, you must make every effort to control how the other participants in the round perceive, interact with, and consider the arguments in the round. This is not easy: you don't have the ability to control the thoughts of the adjudicators or the other debaters. You can, however, influence what others believe the debate is about and, therefore, which arguments they believe are most relevant.

The metaphor of "framing" the round implies that the arguments in the round may be presented in various ways, much like a picture may be displayed in a variety of different frames. How a picture is framed—that is, the color and kind of matting, the material and color of the frame, the ornateness or plainness of the frame, the size of the frame relative to the picture itself, and so forth—will influence how the viewer perceives the image. Similarly, in debate the perspective from which an argument is perceived will influence the audience.

Consider the struggle between antismoking advocates and representatives of the tobacco industry when they argue over regulation of the sale and consumption of cigarettes. The antismoking advocates frame the debate as being about the health of individuals (both smokers and nonsmokers) and the burden on public resources created by the use of tobacco products. The tobacco industry, on the other hand, frames the debate as a conflict over individual liberty and freedom of choice and equates the decision of whether or not to regulate tobacco with other issues of civil liberties. Both sides are right. As the antismoking faction claims, allowing the sale of tobacco products threatens the health of individuals and the well-being of society. However, it's also true that—as the tobacco industry and its supporters claim—limiting access to that product will necessarily diminish individual liberty and freedom of choice. This conflict, like many others, will be won by the side that controls the focus of the debate: what we debate about determines—in large measure—who wins. If we believe this is a debate about individual and public health, those in favor of regulating cigarettes will likely triumph. If we're convinced that this is a debate about civil liberties, we'll likely side with those opposed to increased regulation of cigarettes.

In sum, framing defines the field on which the arguments in a debate will be tested. That field—the argumentative territory in the mind of the adjudicator—is critically important to each team. Like a home-field advantage for a sports team, the ability to argue on one's own terms is a significant advantage for a debate team. Unlike a sports team, however, the ability to define the field of play for arguments in a debate round may mean that the prevailing team not only gets to define the field of play on which the game is contested, but the rules, objectives, and scoring of that game.

Framing may be divided into two types: prospective and retrospective framing. Prospective framing refers to the effort to define the terms of the debate at the beginning of the round (or at the beginning of that team's turn, in British Parliamentary debating). Retrospective framing occurs when a debater summarizes and recasts his arguments in relation to those of his opponents. Though this is the primary focus of the speeches later in a debate round, retrospective framing may also occur (to a lesser extent) at the end of any of the speeches in a debate.

PROSPECTIVE FRAMING

In a footrace, the goal of the race is always known before the race begins, and at least in the case of standardized events, the goal is always the same: a marathon, for example, is always 26.22 miles long. The notion that a race might start without a specified end point is unusual: even more unusual would be a contest in which the contestants themselves determine the end point.

In a debate, however, contestants define the very course, length, and finish line of the contest. In so doing, debaters must not only make their best effort to capture the most territory in the mind of their adjudicators, they must also advance arguments to justify the very size, boundaries, and existence of that territory.

Prospective framing is this contest over the territory of debate. At times, the contest is not very significant: both teams may—explicitly or implicitly—agree on the terms of the debate and simply contest the issues as they follow from those terms. At other times, however, the contest over the ground of the debate is the most significant point of contention between teams; when, by prevailing on the terms of the debate, the team essentially guarantees their victory in the round, the contest over how the debate is framed is essential (consider the above example of which side gets to define the controversy over regulating cigarettes).

Prospective framing typically takes one of two forms: teams may prospectively frame a round by identifying the question posed by the motion or by defining the terms in the debate.

Identifying the question posed by the motion refers to the effort to determine the heart of the controversy implied by the motion. Effectively determining the question not only offers the advantage of setting the ground for the debate but, if done well, clarifies the proposition as the primary point of stasis over which the Proposition and Opposition teams will disagree.[19] Consider the motion "Minors seeking an abortion should be required to have the consent of their parents." This motion contains a variety of potential propositions: the debate could be about whether or not abortion is desirable or undesirable public policy. It could concern whether minors are capable of making rational decisions concerning the termination of a pregnancy. Or the debate could turn on whether parents are the best (or necessary or only) choice of person to act on the child's behalf. Any of these points of stasis may be fruitful areas of inquiry; some are more advantageous to one side of the debate than the other. A winning team will first need to determine which focus it wants to adopt and then convince the audience that its focus is preferable.

Defining the terms of the debate is another form of prospective framing that will influence the ground on which the debate is contested. Consider the motion "This house would ban smoking." Depending on the definition of its terms, this motion could address a smoking ban in a particular place, such as bars and restaurants, or it could focus on banning smoking in all public places, indoor and out. Finally, a legitimate interpretation of this motion may be to ban all smoking, essentially reducing cigarettes to an illicit substance. The ground for this debate — the frame in which the debate will be considered — typically depends on how the Opening Proposition defines the terms. Remember, though, that the Opening Opposition can either contest these terms or define their ground through a "team line," a position that illuminates the ground they plan to defend.

Either of these strategies is likely to appear early in a debater's speech and then be reinforced by the arguments made throughout the speech. Not surprisingly, these efforts at prospective framing are most evident in each team's first speaker's speech.

RETROSPECTIVE FRAMING

Retrospective framing, on the other hand, is most prevalent in the final speeches of the round (also known as the Whip speeches). Responsible for the summary of each side's positions, the Whip speakers are charged with recasting the round and the arguments made by each side in a light most favorable to their side. As the name implies, retrospective framing involves looking back over the round from a particular perspective. Three considerations are key to effective retrospective framing.

First, effective retrospective framing requires the debater to identify the most germane issues in the round. Fundamentally, those issues that are most germane are those material to answering the question the motion posed. Identifying those issues requires that you see the whole round—your arguments and those of your opponents—objectively. Thinking like an adjudicator is one of the secrets of successful debaters. Unfortunately, beyond time spent "behind the pen" as an adjudicator, there is no secret way to acquire an adjudicator's eye for arguments. If the holistic, objective assessment of a round doesn't produce a clear consensus of the most critical issues, you may have to default to other standards of relevance: you may be able to convince the adjudicator that the most critical issues are those that were most hotly contested or those most favorable to your position and strategy. In any case, identifying relevant issues demotes other issues to a less relevant status in the round. Consequently you must carefully select those issues that the adjudicators will also believe to be most important.

Retrospective framing also requires that you consider the organization of the issues you will present. You can use several standards for determining the order in which issues should be addressed: you may prefer to deal with the most critical issues first or last, you may recognize that some issues must be dealt with before other issues are considered, or you may simply want to position issues advantageous to your side or team more prominently in the speech. In any case, prioritizing issues requires that you communicate to the adjudicators that not all issues are equal.

Finally, once you have selected the issues and organized them properly, you need to demonstrate that your arguments have prevailed in each case or, if they haven't, to show that the issue is less significant than other issues in which you have prevailed. This process requires you to analyze who won each issue and determine how those issues interact to prove the proposition true or false.

These recommendations on prospective and retrospective framing are only a starting point to mastering the art of framing. Successful framing depends, in large part, on your ability to identify and structure the arguments exchanged in the round within issues.

Framing the Round by Structuring Issues

All too often debaters pay little attention to the holistic structure of the round and fail to consider where their arguments collide with those of their opponents over identifiable points of stasis. Rest assured, though, that your adjudicators are looking for these points of stasis. It is within these issues that the debate is contested.

What typically happens in a debate is that debaters, obsessed with their own contributions, focus too heavily on their own arguments and either fail to adequately consider and address their opponents' arguments or recognize how their arguments interact with their opponents'. Put more simply, these debaters miss the forest of the debate (the issue-by-issue consideration of the interactions between the various arguments in the round) for the trees (their own individual or team's contribution).

To a certain extent, being aware of the function and importance of framing a round—prospectively or retrospectively—helps to combat this error. By itself, however, knowing that you must frame is not enough; you need to (re)cast the round in a series of issues that both encapsulate the various arguments presented and serve your own strategy of control.

A good metaphor for (re)casting issues is that of housekeeping. Every home becomes messy from our daily living: we leave clothes on the floor, books on the table, and gardening equipment in the yard. Similarly, debate rounds frequently get messy. With eight debaters, each of whom is introducing new material into the round, the mess likely can't be avoided.

But like a house—which benefits from a good straightening up every once in a while—a debate can be made clearer and more efficient if the participants attend to the holistic structure of the round. We tidy up a messy house by returning our things to the places they belong: clothes go into the laundry or back in the closet; books go back on the bookshelf; and our gardening equipment is returned to the shed where our other tools are kept. At the end of a cleaning, the house is a more efficient and orderly place to be: to find a shirt, you go to the closet; books are on the bookshelf, not strewn around the living room, and so on.

Debates also benefit from an on-going effort to tidy up the arguments in the round. Beyond making the debate clearer and the comparison of competing arguments more efficient, grouping arguments with other, like arguments can also serve a strategic function.

In general, your effort to group like arguments is an exercise in defining the issues in which those arguments are contested.[20] As discussed in Chapter 3, the issues in the round are constructs: they are the product of the debaters' efforts to draw boundaries around the territory in which their arguments interact. In general, this effort is an exercise in identifying an appropriate level of abstraction for the issue. As you have learned, an issue must be sufficiently broad so as to be inclusive of the arguments pertaining to it but it must also be narrow enough to allow the meaningful consideration of arguments within that issue.

In his treatment of language, linguist S. I. Hayakawa discussed an "abstraction ladder" of language.[21] Hayakawa's ladder metaphor explained how the level of abstraction in the language we use reflects how we order our understanding of the world around us. Hayakawa's famous example was of how one could use language with varying degrees of abstraction (or specificity) to talk about a cow. Depending on the goal of the communicative act, when referring to that cow, the speaker will choose between language at various levels of abstraction.

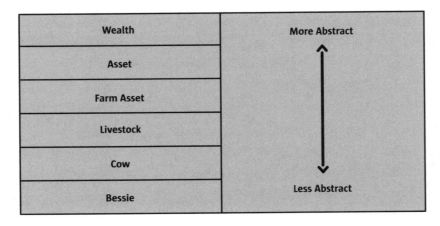

In much the same way, you can create an issue that captures the points of stasis between competing arguments by identifying the appropriate level of abstraction for that issue. Just as our discussion of a cow may utilize language at different levels of abstraction to meet a particular goal, the language we use to describe our arguments also utilizes varying levels of abstraction. Consider a debate about legalizing prostitution, in which the proponents argue that the illegal status of prostitution creates a circumstance in which prostitutes are unable to seek recourse for crimes committed against them. This circumstance, argues the proponent of legalization, leads to unchecked violence against prostitutes.

The specific argument about violence against prostitutes is contained in the category of arguments about the general lack of legal recourse for prostitutes. The more general category of "legal recourse" may include arguments about violence but may also include arguments about fraud committed against prostitutes because of a lack of legal recourse. Similarly, the arguments in the category of "legal recourse" are only one type of argument in the broader category of "equality," a category that may concern—in addition to those arguments about equality of legal recourse—arguments about equality of economic opportunities. The abstraction continues until the most general level—all those arguments available to the Proposition team—is reached.

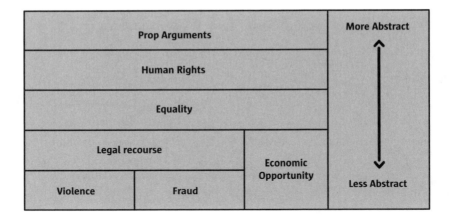

Capturing the arguments made in a debate within issues that give structure and coherence to those arguments is challenging for even experienced debaters. The ability to do so, however, is crucial to successful debating. Controlling the issues under consideration allows you to control the structure of the round and, therefore, control the attention of the adjudicators. One effective way to identify and define issues is to seek a common theme that runs through the arguments. These themes—which serve as the issues that organize the arguments in a round—are broad, unifying topics that serve as an umbrella for the arguments. Identifying issues in a debate begins with finding a description of those arguments that is suitably abstract to contain the arguments while specific enough to have meaning and weight in the round.

Consider the example of the debate over banning smoking in public. The first speaker for the Proposition team may advocate for such a ban by building a case around the following individual arguments, in this order:

1. Second-hand smoke is a serious public health hazard.

2. Smokers create a significantly larger burden on the public health system than do nonsmokers.

3. Nonsmokers have a right to avoid second-hand smoke in public places.

The first speaker for the Opposition may respond with her own set of arguments:

A. Smokers will still continue to smoke; they'll merely do so in private places.

B. Banning smoking in public places will have serious consequences for retailers who depend on the sale of tobacco products.

C. Bars and restaurants will see a decline in patronage from their smoking customers.

D. Smokers have a right to exercise their choice in public.

The third speaker in the debate—the second speaker for the Proposition—has a choice to make: she may either approach the debate as a series of independent arguments made by alternating Proposition and Opposition speakers or she can seek to unify the consideration of those arguments into issues that represent the stasis that naturally exists between those arguments. Gathering the relevant arguments within explicitly identified issues will make the arguments from the Proposition and the Opposition side easier for the adjudicator to understand and compare.

In the above example, the arguments may be gathered into issues as follows:

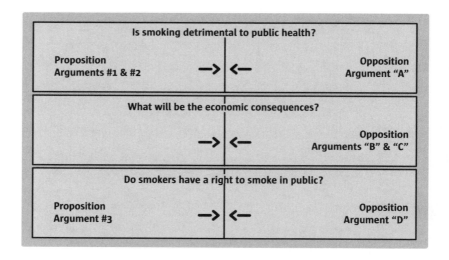

Now, in addition to advancing the arguments that benefit her side, the second Proposition speaker has taken control of the structure of the round by recasting the arguments around points of stasis over which those arguments clash. These issues make it easier for her to control the adjudicator's focus, to compare her team's arguments to those of the Opposition, and to argue for the relative importance of each of the issues. Clearly, controlling the issues in the round presents her with a significant advantage.

CHAPTER 5

The Speakers and Speeches

The British Parliamentary Format

The British Parliamentary academic debating format is the official format of the World Universities Debating Championships (WUDC). As the name suggests, the format has its roots in the British House of Commons, which served as a model for academic debating in British universities. Since its adoption by the WUDC, the format has spread around the world and is now the most widely practiced format of intercollegiate debating.

Like other formats of academic debating, British Parliamentary (BP) debating involves teams that argue for or against a motion before a panel of expert adjudicators. The teams' assignments (for or against the motion), like the motion itself, are provided to the teams by the tournament organizers.

Most formats of academic debating—particularly those known to American audiences—involve only two teams: one team argues for the topic and the other argues against it. The outcome of these debates is binary: at the end of the debate the adjudicators award the win to one of the teams and the loss to the other. Unlike binary formats of debating, BP involves four independent teams per round: two who argue in favor of the motion (known as the Proposition teams) and two who argue against the motion (known as the Opposition teams). Rather than competing for a simple win or loss, each of the teams competes against the others for a ranking at the end of the round.

This approach to debating—that competing teams could share a position of advocacy—initially may be confusing to those familiar with binary forms of academic debating. The explanation for this approach may be found in a version of parliamentary government on which the BP format is modeled. While binary forms of debate are rooted in a judicial model of competing advocacy (as in a criminal court where the accused is argued to be guilty by the prosecution and not guilty by the defense), the BP format employs a legislative model in which parties with different but complimentary interests cooperate to advance the same proposition.[22] This model is grounded in those parliamentary systems of government that utilize a proportionally representational electoral system, in which various parties must form coalitions to establish a governing majority. In these systems, a Green Party may cooperate with a Labor Party to form a government and pass legislation. The Green Party's motives are concern for the environment and the Labor Party's motives are concerns for workers, but both cooperate to advocate for change.

The teams on each side in a BP round cooperate using a very similar approach. Two teams, known as the Opening Proposition and Closing Proposition, are responsible for arguing on behalf of the topic, known as a motion in BP debating. Two more teams—the Opening Opposition and Closing Opposition—are responsible for arguing against the motion. Each of these teams is comprised of two debaters, each of whom has a unique name in the debate.

Opening Proposition	Opening Opposition
1. Prime Minister	2. Leader Opposition
3. Deputy Prime Minister	4. Deputy Leader Opposition
Closing Proposition	**Closing Opposition**
5. Member Proposition	6. Member Opposition
7. Proposition Whip	8. Opposition Whip

Each debater gives one 7-minute speech in a BP round, beginning with the first speaker for the Opening Proposition (the Prime Minister) and alternating between the Proposition and Opposition until each debater has spoken:

Order	Team	Speaker	Speaking
1	Opening Proposition	Prime Minister (PM)	7 minutes
2	Opening Proposition	Leader Opposition (LO)	7 minutes
3	Opening Proposition	Deputy Prime Minister (DPM)	7 minutes
4	Opening Proposition	Deputy Leader Opposition (DLO)	7 minutes
5	Closing Proposition	Member Proposition (MP)	7 minutes
6	Closing Proposition	Member Opposition (MO)	7 minutes
7	Closing Proposition	Proposition Whip (PW)	7 minutes
8	Closing Proposition	Opposition Whip (OP)	7 minutes

During each of these speeches, debaters from the opposite side may ask for the opportunity to interrupt the speaker. Known as Points of

Information (or POIs), these interjections are short questions or statements taken at the discretion of the debater holding the floor. A debater may request the opportunity to present a Point of Information (either verbally or by rising) from a speaker on the opposite side of the motion at any time after the first minute and before the last minute of any speech. The debater holding the floor may accept or refuse POIs at her discretion. If accepted, the debater asking the POI has approximately 15 seconds to make a statement or ask a question. During the Point of Information, the speaking time continues to run. Following the POI, the primary speaker resumes her speech and is expected to integrate her response to the POI into her speech. Debaters are judged on their efforts (successful or not) to offer POIs and to respond to POIs.

With this basic overview of the round in place, I'll now turn to a detailed analysis of each of the speaking positions in the round and consider each speaker's responsibilities to engage in *construction, deconstruction*, and *framing*. To illustrate some of the concepts discussed, I'll track how a debate on the motion *"This house would ban capital punishment"* might unfold.

The Prime Minister's Speech

As the first speech in the round, the Prime Minister's (PM) speech bears a special burden: It must lay out a case that not only offers an argument (or arguments) for the motion but also outlines the round in a way that makes the participation of the other teams feasible.

FRAMING

The PM's most important obligation is to prospectively frame the debate so the other debaters and the adjudicators understand its context and focus. Most often, the motion for BP debates involves a pseudo-legislative policy motion, such as "This house would ban capital punishment" or "India should be granted a permanent seat on the UN Security Council."

The PM has a technical obligation to provide clarity to the debate by offering a *proposition*. To understand the round—that is, for an Opposition team to direct the appropriate attacks against the case/motion, for a Closing Proposition team to develop an appropriate position in support of the case/motion and for the adjudicators to consider the arguments for and against the case/motion, the participants must reach some shared understanding of what they are arguing about—they must agree on a proposition for the debate. In the case of our hypothetical motion, banning capital punishment, two very different debates would occur if the Opening Proposition chose to advocate a proposition of "banning capital punishment for minors" as opposed to "banning capital punishment in all cases for all crimes" (the latter of these two interpretations is the preferable definition, by the way—more on this later). Defining the proposition in a way that promotes the most substantive, focused, and productive debate is a critical responsibility of the Prime Minister.

In some cases, developing a proposition for the debate requires that the PM provide an extended discussion of how the motion would be implemented. Known as a "model,"[23] and introduced early in the PM's speech (usually immediately after her opening comments), the model outlines the policy considerations and constraints under which the motion will be enacted. The motion "This house would ban smoking" requires that the PM outline the specifics of such a ban. In policy terms, this means that the PM would likely discuss the mandates of a ban ("we would ban the production, sale, and consumption of tobacco in

all forms") and the enforcement of that ban ("violators would be subject to criminal and civil sanctions commensurate with the severity of
the violation, ranging from simple fines for possession to incarceration
for repeated attempts to produce and distribute"). In some cases, the
PM may discuss the agent responsible for implementing the policy, the
financing for the policy and other terms of the policy that would make
clear the intent of the Opening Proposition team.

At other times, meeting the obligation to offer a proposition for the
debate is as simple as defining one or more terms of the motion. Some
motions are so specific that they require little in the way of interpretation: consider the motion *"Public health systems should refuse to provide fertility treatments in situations in which the couples or individual
seeking treatment involves a woman over the age of 42."* In this case,
the terms of the policy addressed by the motion are relatively clear.
Perhaps the PM could detail which fertility treatments would be included in this prohibition or illustrate the type of public health systems
involved by referring to an example of a particular country, though it
seems relatively clear that the motion is written to be inclusive of all
treatments and applicable to health systems involving universal health
care provided by public money.

Though the PM has the technical obligation of providing a proposition for the debate, the decision of how to define the proposition is a
strategic decision. Generally, that decision should be guided by consideration of how the adjudicators will evaluate the effort to define the
proposition. Specifically, the PM's effort should be guided by the "better debate" standard. Put simply, when employing the "better debate"
standard the adjudicators ask, "Did the debater's efforts make the debate better?" In the case of the PM, what typically makes for a better

debate is a proposition that is inclusive of the Opposition's potential ground rather than exclusive of it. [24]

Here's where the difference between the "ban capital punishment for minors" and the "ban capital punishment in all cases for all crimes" interpretations become evident. In the former, while the ground the PM has outlined may be more defensible because it is narrower and more limited, it is so only because it excludes potential Opposition ground. An Opposition that prepared for the motion "This house would ban capital punishment" assuming they would be arguing about the broad category of punishments that fall under most common understandings of capital punishment would have to modify or, more likely, discard many of their arguments. Moreover, because the debate about whether minors should be subject to capital punishment occurs on more restricted and narrow territory, it is less likely to provide fertile ground for arguments from the remaining seven debaters in the round.

Let me be clear: a debate about whether or not minors should be subject to capital punishment is timely, compelling, and potentially very interesting. However, given that the debaters were assigned the more general motion of banning *all* capital punishment, restricting the debate to minors seems a decision motivated by a desire for strategic advantage rather than a genuine desire to interrogate the question posed by the motion as presented. Most adjudicators will interpret such a strategy as evasive rather than strategically clever, and evaluate the effort accordingly.[25]

In the end, then, the best framing from the PM is that which makes the debate clearer, creates a concrete proposal that may be defended by the Proposition teams and critiqued by the Opposition teams, and is both faithful to the motion and likely to lead to a "better" debate.

Constructive Argumentation

In the majority of cases, the PM's framing effort takes only 1 to 1½ minutes of the PM's speech. By far the most significant portion of the PM's time is dedicated to the development of the constructive arguments that offer reasons for the proposition he has developed in his framing. That constructive effort is the product of considered analysis and synthesis of potential arguments for the proposition. Typically, the PM will offer three to four arguments for the proposition. These points may be independent or logically progressive, but they will certainly comprise a complete, varied, and thorough set of proof for the proposition. For more on constructing effective arguments, please refer to the discussion of constructive argumentation in Chapter 3

Deconstructive Argumentation

The majority of PM speeches don't focus on deconstructive argumentation for one simple reason: as the first speech in the round, there is not yet an opposing effort to deconstruct. That said, some PMs make use of techniques that anticipate and preemptively critique anticipated arguments. This strategy should be used selectively. Though the PM may gain the advantage by undercutting the credit given to the speaker who introduces an argument, putting the Opposition on the defensive and directing the Opposition's attention from their intended strategy to one defined by the Proposition, the potential risk is considerable. Many a PM has inadvertently provided an opponent with an argument that she hadn't thought of and one that adjudicators later favor.

The PM Speech in the Capital Punishment Debate

In our hypothetical debate, the PM opts to define the motion as broadly as possible to promote a thorough interrogation of the question implied by the motion. After offering a simple model that makes clear who will ban capital punishment (all nations who wish to remain members of the UN), for which crimes the ban will apply (for all crimes, in all circumstances) and which specifies that even those who have been sentenced to capital punishment but are awaiting execution will be spared by this ban, the PM moves on to offer a case developed around two constructive arguments. First, the PM argues that there is no empirical evidence that capital punishment is a deterrent. States with and without capital punishment tend have similar crime rates. Moreover, notes the PM, a deterrent is not likely for crimes usually subject to capital punishment, such as murder and rape, because they are typically crimes of passion in which the perpetrator does not rationally consider the consequences of his actions. The PM then moves on to develop a second argument concerning the inevitable errors that occur in the application of justice. In the case of capital punishment, such errors — whether the product of misfeasance or malfeasance — cannot be corrected if discovered later. Thus, the PM argues, capital punishment has considerable practical flaws that warrant its elimination.

In the notes of the round, such a speech might be recorded like this:

Prime Minister	Leader Opposition

Model: All UN members cease immediately; convert to life sentences
 	
1. CP doesn't deter crime
    A. No empirical proof
    B. c/n deter crimes of passion
2. Errors irreversible
    A. The system is fallible	

Deputy Prime Minister	**Deputy Leader Opposition**
Member Proposition	**Member Opposition**
Proposition Whip	**Opposition Whip**

The Leader of the Opposition's Speech

If the PM bears the special burden of defining the focus of the round and the overarching strategic focus of both Proposition teams, the Leader of the Opposition (LO) bears at least some of the same burden for the Opposition side. As the first speaker for the Opposition, the LO is responsible for framing the focus of the Opposition teams as well as the introducing the constructive and deconstructive positions of the Opening Opposition team.

FRAMING

The LO faces a decision about how to frame her opponent's arguments. Principally, she must decide whether she will accept or challenge the PM's interpretation of the motion. The decision the LO makes in an overwhelming number of cases is to accept the definition as presented. That said, the issue of "fair" definitions (and, more importantly, how an Opposition team should deal with what they perceive to be an "unfair" definition) typically is of great concern, especially to novice BP debaters. Consequently, I'll spend some time here discussing an approach you'll likely never use. A couple of observations will help to explain the decision of whether or not to challenge a definition.

First, remember that the proposition for the debate is itself subject to debate. The PM's interpretation of a motion is not sacrosanct. His interpretation is no different than his descriptive, relational, or evaluative arguments about the truth of the proposition: it is an argument subject to the same potential errors and worthy of the same critique as any other argument in the round.

Like the PM, the LO is subject to the "better debate" standard. In other words, the decision to challenge a definition must be made with an eye toward the larger consequences for the quality of the round; often the round will be better if the LO chooses to engage a narrow and arguably "unfair" definition by making the best arguments available rather than complaining about the definition offered. Given the tendency of definitional objections to muddy the debate by creating two potential territories on which the debate may be contested, this decision should not be made lightly.

Perhaps this latter observation is why there are so few definitional challenges mounted by LOs and why, of those that are attempted, so few are successful. Certainly in my experience with BP debating — which began with a trip to the World Championships in 1992 — I have not seen a definitional challenge that was executed successfully. In short, Opening Proposition teams overwhelmingly tend to define the terms of the debate with a great deal of fidelity to the motion provided and Opening Opposition teams overwhelmingly tend to accept that approach. It's part of the culture of competitive BP debating.

That said, should an LO think that her best option is a definitional challenge, she would take the following steps. First, the LO must be absolutely certain that her interpretation is more in line with what the question implied by the motion. The most obvious instances are those in which the PM has misunderstood something implied by the motion. Consider a circumstance, for example, in which a PM assigned to defend a ban on capital punishment offers a case advocating that spanking be declared illegal. In this instance, the PM has clearly confused *corporal* punishment with *capital* punishment and offered a case that is largely irrelevant to the intent of the motion.[26]

Once the LO is certain that objecting to the PM's definition is the best strategy, she faces another decision. She now must decide whether to rehabilitate the PM's interpretation or to abandon it. If she chooses to rehabilitate the interpretation, she would use what is known colloquially as the "surely" strategy. This strategy seeks to correct the interpretive error while still leaving open the possibility for the Opening Proposition to rejoin the debate. It is particularly useful when the PM overreaches in the interpretation or makes an error of judgment on the fly, perhaps in response to a challenging POI.

Suppose, for example, the PM proposes banning cigarettes across the board but neglects to discuss how such a prohibition might be enforced. In response to a POI from the Opposition, the PM slips and inadvertently implies that the consequences for using tobacco would be execution of the offender. This is not likely part of the real-world policy discussion about making cigarettes illegal, nor is focusing on such an obvious lapse in what may otherwise be a well-reasoned proposal likely to lead to an interesting and challenging debate. In this case, a wise LO might open her speech with the following framing:

> Surely the PM didn't mean to imply that a first offense of tobacco possession would be punishable by death. That said, the Opening Proposition makes some compelling arguments about why significant criminal sanctions are warranted for those who violate the prohibition. We're going to engage those reasons and prove why attempting to prohibit the personal choice to use tobacco is wrong in principle, regardless of the penalty imposed for those who would violate such a prohibition.

In so doing, the LO avoids what would likely be a lackluster debate about whether smoking warrants the death penalty and focuses instead on the question implied by the motion: is attempting to ban tobacco use a good idea? Most participants—including a savvy Deputy Prime Minister—would recognize that this is a better choice and would follow suit.

The other option for dealing with a poorly interpreted motion is for the LO to reject the interpretation out of hand and offer a case that addresses (what she believes to be) the correct interpretation. Again, I want to emphasize that this would be the preferred option in an exceedingly small minority of situations. Should, however, the LO be convinced that this is her best strategic option, she would do two things to offer a comprehensive objection to the interpretation. First, she would have to explain why the PM's interpretation of the motion is insufficient, inappropriate, or not debatable. Such grounds may include that the interpretation is wholly unrelated to the motion, that the interpretation forces the Opposition to take a morally unsustainable position in the round, or that the PM's proposed proposition is so broadly accepted as true as to be rendered uncontroversial and, therefore, not debatable. Alternately, an objectionable interpretation of a motion might be one for which the debate is constrained to an unreasonable temporal or geographic setting to the exclusion of other, reasonable arguments.[27] Following her explanation of the grounds on which the interpretation should be considered unreasonable, the LO would have to offer her version of the "correct" interpretation of the motion. Typically this is done to demonstrate how far from the actual motion the PM's interpretation has landed.

Once the LO is convinced that the adjudicators accept her version of the motion, her final step is to offer arguments against that version.

Here the LO's focus shifts from arguing against the proposition as offered by the PM to arguing against the motion as the proposition. The consequence of this shift of focus is that the Opening Proposition's case will be left relatively unaddressed by the LO; ignoring your opponents' arguments, is a risky move and I should emphasize once again how rarely this strategy should be adopted.[28]

The final comment I'll offer is one regarding what happens to the rest of the debate following a formal definitional challenge. The rules of the World Universities Debating Championships explain that each subsequent team in the round has the option of following the lead of the LO and pursuing the debate on the terms of the alternate definition without penalty, provided that the PM's definition is legitimately objectionable. The rules also provide the opportunity to the Closing Proposition team to offer another, alternate interpretation of the motion if the (alternate) interpretation offered by the Opening Opposition is objectionable. The same privilege extends to the Closing Opposition should, in this case, the Closing Government's (alternate, alternate) interpretation also prove to be objectionable.[29] As you can imagine, such rounds are painful for all involved and should be avoided at nearly any cost.

If the LO chooses to accept the general proposition for debate as offered by the PM, she still may have some work to do with regard to framing. Often, the Opening Opposition can benefit from developing a "team line," or an articulation of specific ground the Opening Opposition will defend. This ground should be germane to the proposition as accepted by the LO but should provide the Opening Opposition (and, potentially, the Closing Opposition team) the advantage of a more focused effort to counter the Proposition. See the LO speech below for an example of how to frame a useful team line.

DECONSTRUCTIVE ARGUMENTATION

Following her framing efforts, the LO will typically move on to deconstruction by challenging the PM's key arguments. Deconstructive argumentation is a critical focus for the LO (and, indeed, for all subsequent speakers) as the engagement of opposing arguments is the defining characteristic of debating and one of the chief criteria adjudicators use in determining the ranking of teams.

The LO would likely index the arguments made by the PM and respond to each of them in turn. Some LOs choose to offer a single pertinent critique of each argument while others list a number of objections to each of the PM's positions. In either case, the LO's responsibility is to create significant doubt about the strength of the PM's arguments. This entire effort would typically occupy 2 to 3 minutes of the LO's speech.

CONSTRUCTIVE ARGUMENTATION

Like the PM, the LO is expected to develop positive matter in support of her position. This is strategically advantageous to the Opening Opposition team: though it's conceivable that an Opposition's deconstructive effort would be so powerful as to render a Proposition's argument moot (and, therefore, to deliver the win to the Opening Opposition team), such instances are rare. A more judicious strategy is to offer both "arguments against" in the form of deconstructive argumentation and "arguments for" in a constructive effort. Adjudicators are more likely to vote for a team who demonstrates proficiency in all skills rather than concentrating on one. More to the point, the rules of the WUDC advise adjudicators to evaluate each speaker's efforts to introduce "positive matter" into the debate.[30]

The LO's constructive argumentation, like that of the PM, would likely consist of 2 to 4 points that offer independent or logically progressive reasons why the position of the Opening Opposition is credible. This effort — in most speeches — would occupy the bulk of the LO's effort, likely 3 to 4 minutes of her 7 minute speech.

THE LO SPEECH IN THE CAPITAL PUNISHMENT DEBATE

In light of the PM's reasonable interpretation of the motion, our LO (correctly) decides to proceed directly to the deconstruction of the PM's points rather than object to his definition. With regard to the PM's argument that capital punishment is not a deterrent, the LO argues that such an effect is not measurable, because determining who intended to but opted not to commit a crime is impossible. No one, argues the LO, readily admits to wanting to commit a crime, particularly a capital crime, but chooses not to do so only because of the likelihood of sanction. With regard to the PM's argument about the irreversibility of the application of capital punishment, the LO argues that these errors are not intrinsic to capital punishment itself but to the system that determines guilt and assigns punishment. Fix the system, claims the LO, and you eliminate this argument as a reason to do away with capital punishment.

From this basis, the LO proceeds to framing the Opening Opposition's position. Rather than arguing that all crimes, in all cases, may be worthy of capital punishment, the LO chooses to focus the Opposition's effort on proving that capital punishment is a legitimate and desirable consequence for those found guilty of crimes against humanity. Such crimes, argues the LO, are extreme examples of the worst of criminal behavior (indeed, such crimes are defined as those that "shock the conscience") and as such provide a compelling test of the Proposition's stance that capital punishment is not warranted in any case.

To prove that those convicted of crimes against humanity deserve capital punishment, the LO develops two lines of constructive argument. First, she argues that prosecution of crimes against humanity first and foremost seeks justice, and that justice is best served — in this case — by capital punishment. This is so, she contends, because only capital punishment can begin to repay the social debt created by those who are convicted of crimes against humanity. Moreover, she argues that a degree of closure is achieved when someone who has terrorized a population is put to death. Though his acts cannot be redeemed, that person can never again commit such atrocities and the victims are therefore reassured of the end of their torment. As a second line of argument, the LO contends that preserving capital punishment for these crimes would convey an unambiguous moral stance and make clear that the world community will not condone such behavior.

If recorded in the notes of a round, the LO's speech might look like this:

Prime Minister	Leader Opposition

Model: All UN members cease immediately; convert to life sentences
 	
1. CP doesn't deter crime
    A. No empirical proof
    B. c/n deter crimes of passion
2. Errors irreversible
    A. The system is fallible
	Deterrence? Cannot measure effect
	Errors? In application, not in CP itself; fix system
	
	Team Line: Preserve CP for crimes against humanity
	A. Justice demands retribution
	    1. Balance depends on payment of debt
	    2. Provides closure
	B. Need unambiguous moral stance

Deputy Prime Minister	**Deputy Leader Opposition**
Member Proposition	**Member Opposition**
Proposition Whip	**Opposition Whip**

The Deputy Speeches

The next two speeches in the round, as the second speeches of each of the opening teams, are functionally similar. Their primary focus is to support the effort of their partner while contributing to the advancement of the arguments in the round. The Deputy Prime Minister's and the Deputy Leader Opposition's responsibilities, like those of their partners, may be considered in terms of framing, deconstructive argumentation, and constructive argumentation.

FRAMING

If the PM has offered a reasonable interpretation of the motion and the LO has accepted that interpretation, the framing responsibilities of the Deputy speakers will be different than those of their opening partners. Their concern is not with determining the proposition for the round but with directing which issues will be paramount in the appraisal of that proposition. In other words, ideally at this point in the debate, the teams have agreed to the proposition even if they haven't yet agreed on which arguments are most relevant to testing it.

When teams contest a proposition, they do so by considering issues material to determining the truth or falsity of that motion. Which issues are material and what relative attention those issues should be accorded are as legitimate a focus of the debate as is who prevails on a particular issue.[31] Typically, the effort to direct the adjudicators' attention toward particular issues while diminishing others becomes more evident in the Deputy speeches.

The Deputies may take two general approaches to this effort: they may explicitly compare and contrast the issues in play in an effort to emphasize their preferred issue or they may, more subtly, begin to group arguments in the round into issues that address the proposition in their favor.

The explicit effort is preferable if the opening speakers have already defined very clear issues. For example, if the PM builds a case around a general theme, such as the economic reasons to accept the proposition, and the LO responds by offering a constructive effort built around the cultural reasons to reject the proposition, the Deputies will likely benefit from adopting this structure and proceeding directly to the prioritization of one of these reasons over the other (the Deputy Prime Minister would provide reasons why, for example, economic reasons should be considered over cultural reasons).

More frequently, however, identifying and prioritizing issues take the second approach. When the opening debaters have not explicity identified clear issues around which their individual arguments coalesce, the Deputy Speakers may gain ground by staking out this territory and grouping competing arguments into these issues. Consider a round in which each preceding speaker—the PM and the LO—has offered three to four independent arguments for her positions, none of which directly clash with others. A savvy Deputy may be able to reduce the number of arguments the adjudicator must consider by combining some of these arguments into broader issues. This approach, when done well, has two advantages: it is an opportunity to emphasize certain (preferred) arguments while diminishing the attention on others and it allows the Deputy to (re)cast the round in more simple, hopefully stable, terms that will persist throughout the remainder of the debate (ideally because the Closing teams will adopt the new structure in their consideration of the round). An example of this latter approach may be seen in the Deputy speeches in the capital punishment round below.

DECONSTRUCTIVE ARGUMENTATION

Like the choice made by the LO, the Deputies have to decide how to structure their speech with regard to the placement of the framing and deconstructive efforts. For some Deputies, the framing effort — which, as discussed above, is more about shaping arguments that already exist than directing the anticipated proposition for the debate — becomes intertwined with the deconstructive effort. If, for example, the Deputy speaker opts to group the various arguments in the round into broader issues for the adjudicators' consideration, the deconstruction of their opponents' arguments in each of those issues will occur while this new frame for the round is unfolding (as will, of course, the reconstruction of the first speaker's arguments and construction of any new arguments on behalf of the Deputy's team's position).

If, however, the Deputy opts to deal with the material (particularly the new constructive material) presented by the preceding speaker independent of any effort to reframe those arguments into issues — which many effective Deputy speakers do — she would deal with deconstruction in much the same way the earlier speakers did: she would engage in deconstructive argumentation before moving to constructive argumentation and utilize the standard "ICE" structure for the refutation of each of the preceding speaker's arguments.

CONSTRUCTIVE ARGUMENTATION

The Deputy speakers, more than any other speakers in the round, have a unique challenge with regard to their constructive effort: they are charged with sustaining their team's position in the round, fulfilling the mandate of the rules to offer unique positive matter, and reconstructing those arguments offered by their partners that may have been compromised by their opponents' deconstructive efforts. Fortunately, the Deputy has a variety of tools at his or her disposal that make overcoming these challenges manageable.

Chief among these tools is the previously discussed strategy of recasting the round in issues that are inclusive of the arguments being exchanged between the teams. This approach, when combined with the deconstruction of opposing arguments, can be a powerful way to locate a constructive effort in territory where those arguments will do the most good. By combining an effort to frame the debate around the newly identified issues with the deconstruction of the opposing arguments and reconstruction of the first speaker's arguments, the Deputy speaker not only controls the focus and direction of the round but the treatment of each of the arguments relevant to each of the issues that provide the focus and direction.

Beyond this approach, the reconstruction of arguments that belong to the Deputy's team deserves special attention. The forward motion of the debate requires that each speaker not only add new material to the round, but that each speaker also address the opposing team's deconstruction of her team's arguments. This is particularly true for the Deputy speakers, after whom the debate will continue for at least four more speeches by two completely different (and competing) teams. The danger, of course, is that the arguments by the Opening teams may be mischaracterized or—perhaps worse—ignored. Shoring up the team's position to sustain through others' efforts is the responsibility of the Deputy speakers. An effective Deputy speaker will address directly the critique of critical arguments by the preceding speaker, offer new analysis and evidence to resubstantiate the line of argument advanced by her partner and reposition those arguments to be most supportive of her team's overall strategy. Like other constructive efforts, this endeavor should be the final area of focus: the Deputy speaker should end his or her speech with the adjudicators firmly planted in his or her team's territory.

If the Deputy speaker moves the debate forward with her effort to reconcile the deconstruction of her opponent's arguments with the reconstruction of her team's positions, she has likely met the mandate of contributing positive matter to the round. Some Deputy speakers, though, feel more comfortable if their constructive contribution is an explicitly distinct area of argumentation, often previewed by their partners but reserved for the second speaker to develop. Known as a *split*, this technique requires the first speaker of a team to forecast not only the points he will make in his speech but to announce that his partner — the Deputy speaker — will have a distinct, novel constructive point offered anew in her speech. The Deputy speaker then proceeds to live up to this prediction by developing this new substantive point. If, for example, a Leader Opposition develops an economic and security argument against a particular motion, she may announce that her partner will be responsible for developing a cultural argument against the motion.

I've never been a fan of the split for two reasons: first, reserving a point for the second speaker makes the effort by the primary speaker on a team appear incomplete. Minimally, the reservation of a substantive argument suggests that the constructive effort by the first speaker is inadequate; in the worst case, such an approach can leave the impression that the team is presenting a "hung" case (one that doesn't develop the entirety of its proof) or that certain quality arguments are being sandbagged for the later speech when the team's opponents will be less able to refute those arguments. The second reason I dislike the split tactic is that so many speakers get married to a tactic or argument in preparation time and lose the ability to respond to the round as it develops. Because they spent time creating their own point, and because their partner told the audience that the split would be forthcoming, the Deputy speaker is highly inclined to present her split, regardless of whether it's still relevant in the debate (or whether, even if relevant, time would be better spent elsewhere).

In my opinion, a far better strategy is to present a complete case and develop in Deputy speakers the potential supporting material that may be used to repair or extend the case and the instincts to know when, where, and how to use that material.

THE DPM SPEECH IN THE CAPITAL PUNISHMENT DEBATE

Our Deputy Prime Minister (DPM) opens her speech with a deconstructive effort that first considers the team line advanced by the LO. In this case, the DPM's response is little more than a clarification: she makes clear the point of stasis at which the positions advocated by the Opening Proposition and Opposition meet: the Opening Proposition will maintain that capital punishment should not be an option in any case, including crimes against humanity (identified as "CAH" in the notes below). This cements the positions of each team in the round and effectively ends the possibility for any later debate over the interpretations of the motion: this debate will be about whether we should prohibit capital punishment in general or preserve the punishment option at least for crimes against humanity.

From here, the DPM moves on to deconstruct the LO's constructive arguments. Instead of taking the LO's two independent positions separately, the DPM chooses to group both of the arguments under one heading: justice. Justice, she claims, may only be realized in a context where the state maintains moral authority. By utilizing capital punishment, the DPM claims, the state relinquishes its moral authority because it engages in the taking of life. Particularly where the state seeks retribution (the first argument about justice offered by the LO), this moral authority is compromised by the desire of the state to "get even" with the criminal. The DPM claims that the moral uncertainty inherent in capital punishment calls into question the ability of the state to administer justice. This uncertainty is in direct contradiction with the LO's claims about the need for an unambiguous moral stance.

The tactic of grouping all of the opposing team's arguments under a broad issue sets up the DPM to position those arguments against the arguments offered by her team. In doing so, the DPM is establishing the issue of "justice" against which the Opening Proposition's broad issue of "practical concerns" may be positioned.

From this combined deconstructive and framing effort, the DPM transitions to the reconstruction of her team's arguments. Under the title of "practical concerns prevent justice" — another effort to position the arguments against each other within a broad issue — the DPM first reconsiders the arguments her partner offered: that there exists no evidence of deterrence and that errors in the administration of capital punishment are rampant. In doing so she responds to the deconstructive effort of the LO and attempts to rehabilitate her partner's arguments. Finally, to offer another area of support for the broad claim that the administration of capital punishment is rife with practical problems, the DPM addresses the racism inherent in the application of capital punishment, particularly in the United States. The number of minorities subject to capital punishment is disproportionate to the number of minorities in broader society. This, the DPM argues, is an inherent feature of capital punishment and another reason to reject it.

As recorded, the DPM's speech may look like this:

Prime Minister	Leader Opposition
Model: All UN members cease immediately; convert to life sentences	**Deterrence**? Cannot measure effect **Errors**? In application, not in CP itself; fix system

1. CP doesn't deter crime
    A. No empirical proof
    B. c/n deter crimes of passion
2. Errors irreversible
    A. The system is fallible
	Team Line: Preserve CP for crimes against humanity
	A. Justice demands retribution
	    1. Balance depends on payment of debt
	    2. Provides closure
	B. Need unambiguous moral stance

Deputy Prime Minister	Deputy Leader Opposition
CAH? should prohibit in all cases **Justice**? Exists only with fair application of laws	

1. Practical concerns prevent justice
    A. No deterrence: no evidence of success
    B. Errors rampant, compromise justice
    C. Racist application	

Member Proposition	Member Opposition
Proposition Whip	Opposition Whip

THE DLO SPEECH IN THE CAPITAL PUNISHMENT DEBATE

The effort to combine deconstruction and framing is most evident in the speech of the Deputy Leader Opposition (DLO). Recognizing the clarity offered by contrasting practical concerns with the principle of justice, the DLO opens his speech by explicitly comparing the two issues. First, in response to the DPM's claim that justice is unachievable in a system of imperfectly administered laws, the DLO argues that the perfectly equitable application of laws is not a precondition to the pursuit of justice. In fact, argues the DLO, it's more likely that the pursuit of justice precedes the effort to make the application of laws equitable, given that the pursuit of principles guides the practical choices we make. Moreover, the DLO argues that the fact that the system of administration may be improved does not establish the claim that capital punishment is unjust. The problems with capital punishment detailed by the Opening Proposition are problems of administration, not problems with the punishment itself. The answer to an imperfect system is to fix the system, not to abandon the punishment.

From comparing practical and justice issues, the DLO devotes the remainder of his speech to reestablishing the argument that justice requires crimes against humanity be punished with execution. Initially he claims that balance and clarity are served by executing criminals convicted of crimes against humanity, reestablishing arguments made by the LO. He closes his speech by offering an analysis of how the pursuit of justice is grounded in a practical effort to improve the human condition. By arguing that acting in accordance with the ideal of justice produces very tangible results, the DLO is attempting to capture some of the territory staked out by the Opening Proposition team by meeting the arguments about the "real world" application of capital punishment made by the Opening Proposition with an opposing argument that attempts to demonstrate the "real world" reasons for pursuing justice.

The DLO's speech might be recorded as follows:

Prime Minister	Leader Opposition
Model: All UN members cease immediately; convert to life sentences	**Deterrence**? Cannot measure effect **Errors**? In application, not in CP itself; fix system
1. CP doesn't deter crime	**Team Line**: Preserve CP for crimes
A. No empirical proof	against humanity
B. c/n deter crimes of passion	**A.** Justice demands retribution
2. Errors irreversible	1. Balance depends on
A. The system is fallible	payment of debt
	2. Provides closure
	B. Need unambiguous moral stance

Deputy Prime Minister	Deputy Leader Opposition
CAH? should prohibit in all cases	**Practical vs. Justice?**
Justice? Exists only with fair application of laws	A. Justice is an ideal; strive even if not perfect
	B. System can be improved; doesn't prove CP unjust
1. Practical concerns prevent justice	
A. No deterrence: no evidence of success	**Justice**
B. Errors rampant, compromise justice	A. Need balance & clarity
C. Racist application	B. CP for CAH = improve the human condition

Member Proposition	Member Opposition

Proposition Whip	Opposition Whip

The Member Speeches

The Member speeches offer the first opportunities for the closing teams to develop their positions. As discussed earlier, the role of the closing teams is analogous to that of a political party that shares a co-alition majority with other political parties in a legislative body: while they may cooperate with other political parties to establish a governing majority that can create policy, they likely are motivated to do so by an agenda different from that of the other party. These separate interests maintain distinctions between those political parties, even though they cooperate to achieve a shared goal.

In a BP round, the four teams compete independently for ranking in the close of the round. Consequently, each team must distinguish themselves not only from the opposing teams but from the other team on their bench. Establishing a unique argumentative identity is critical to making clear to the adjudicators why a particular team should be preferred to others. For closing teams, this effort is most evident in the constructive argumentation offered by the first speaker for each of the closing teams. In fact, this effort is so important to the success of the closing team that the product of that effort, known as an "extension," has become a widely accepted expectation; the Member's attempt to develop his or her team's identity in the round is subject to intense scrutiny by the adjudicators.

Though the closing teams share the same threefold division of re-sponsibilities as the opening teams (framing-deconstructing-construct-ing), the emphasis of the Member speaker is most heavily focused on the extension, which, as the description of the strategy suggests, is largely constructive. That said, an effective extension is also an effort to redirect (or at least reposition) the attention of the adjudicators in the round and, as such, involves attention to how the round is framed. Moreover, an extension must be germane to the arguments made by the opposing teams and, as such, involves deconstructive argumentation.

Compelling Member speakers may opt to either separate these ef-forts or to combine them into their extension. If the Member separates the framing, deconstruction, and construction, the approach is much like that employed by the preceding speakers: the Member speaker decides how to cast his team's effort in the round, critiques the arguments of her opponents in that context and then proceeds to the positive matter she'll introduce into the round. Most often, Member speakers dispatch with any necessary deconstruction first, then turn their attention to reframing the round in terms of the constructive argumentation in their extension.

THE EXTENSION

Balancing an effort to establish a unique argumentative identity with the obligation to continue a general direction of advocacy introduced by a team against which you're competing is a delicate matter; those teams who are able to do so effectively are typically those who appreciate the unique ability of the BP format to interrogate thoroughly a controversial topic. By expecting the last two teams in the round to discover and advance novel arguments in the round while integrating that effort with the positions of the preceding teams, the format sets the stage for a debate marked by a variety of perspectives integrated into a thorough analysis of the question before the house.

The approach embraced by these closing teams and, particularly, by the Member speakers, may be described as "coopertition." Coopertition implies that that the closing team is simultaneously engaged in cooperation and competition with their opening team.

A brief aside about adjudicating BP debates is relevant here. One of the most challenging aspects of adjudicating BP debates is quite simply remembering who said what over the course of the 56-minute round. This fundamental challenge is the concern not only of the adjudicator but also debaters who recognize that they share in the responsibility for making their team's arguments memorable. This is particularly critical for closing teams, where they don't have a truly "blank slate" on which to construct their arguments but must position their efforts in the context of (and, indeed, in concert with) their competitors' arguments. Establishing a unique identity, therefore, must be a primary concern for a closing team. This observation also substantiates another note of advice: effective extensions are those that are singular in their focus. In other words, a team is easier to remember if they are noteworthy for a particular, unique, and simple reason. If a team employs a scattergun approach to argument, remembering all of their reasons is not as likely. Find a unifying theme for the extension — or simply choose only a single argument around which to build the extension — and you'll likely be rewarded for it.

Generally, extensions fall into three broad categories: they may offer a new line of argument, examine a particular piece of evidence to ground abstract arguments in tangible support, or provide greater depth and analysis on a line of argument that already exists.

Establishing a new line of argument offers the clearest example of meeting the strategic priorities inherent in offering an extension. Developing a unique argument identity is most easily accomplished by focusing your attention on constructing an argument that is uniquely the property of your team. If, for example, the opening teams focused their arguments on the economic and cultural analysis of the motion, a closing team may distinguish themselves by concentrating on the legal aspects of the decision. In so doing, they spend their time on territory not yet covered in the debate and are more likely to remain distinct in the mind of the adjudicators.

While the Member speakers are seeking to distinguish themselves from the opening teams, they must not abandon the opening teams, either by deviating from the general direction of the opening team's argument (known as "knifing" and discussed below) or neglecting the opening team's arguments. An effective Member speaker does not introduce an entirely new debate in the latter half of the round but, ideally, integrates a new element of the broader debate with the general flow of the debate as it has played out so far. In other words, an effective Member speaker must be considerate of and responsive to what has come before.

Another approach to the extension — and one that more clearly satisfies the priority of maintaining consistency with the opening teams — is the effort to examine a specific piece of evidence that supports the general arguments of the opening team. Often this approach has the Member speaker developing the details of a case study in which the general principles and arguments advocated by the opening teams are placed into more tangible context. By taking the time to "unpack" an actual occurrence, the Member speaker provides depth and specificity to the case that — if such an in-depth approach were offered in an opening speech — might have been seen as too limited in scope to justify the proposition. This second approach is not limited to case studies, though development of detailed narratives can be a very effective way to establish proof for an argument. Statistical analyses, testimony of authoritative sources, and the like may also provide material for this type of an extension. Regardless of the type of evidence examined, the second approach is characterized by the Member speaker's concentration on one piece of evidence in an effort to illuminate the exceptionality of that evidence.

Finally, an extension may be developed around adding depth to an opening team's line of argument. This approach, on its face, seems to contradict the basic tenet guiding the development of extensions: that the extension develops a unique argumentative identity for the closing team. In reality, there will be times when a Member speaker (or the Member in cooperation with her Whip partner) can think of no unique contribution to the round. These times will typically occur when the opening team has attempted to cover "every" argument for their position. In these cases, when it's likely that the effort to cover so much ground means that some arguments don't get the treatment they deserve in the opening team's speeches, the member can create an extension by adding substance, analysis, and support to an underdeveloped argument. Keep in mind that of the three approaches, this is the most risky: inattentive adjudicators (or an unclear effort on the part of the Member to distinguish the closing team's contribution) risks giving undue credit to the team who introduced the argument into the round.

In general, extensions, and debaters' efforts to establish them, suffer from three challenges: "burnt turf," failure to distinguish, and "knifing." These problems are listed in order, from the least severe to the most troublesome.

The burnt turf problem results when an opening team covers "all" the arguments that may be made about a particular issue. I place the word "all" in quotation marks to imply that this problem is seldom created by the actual coverage of every possible argument that may be made for a particular proposition; it is more likely the result of the Member speaker's lack of knowledge on the subject or lack of imagination about the potential arguments that may be made.

The best response to a burnt turf situation is for the Member to do his best to carve out a unique argumentative identity with whatever resources are available to him. Sometimes that means adopting the second approach to an extension and developing, in detail, an article of evidence that supports that team's position on the proposition. At other times, the best a Member speaker can do is to adopt a line of argument already introduced into the round by a preceding team and to "give it legs" by deepening the focus, analysis, or support for that argument.

Failure to distinguish is a strategic problem marked by a failure of the Member speaker to make clear the difference between the opening and closing teams. Typically, this problem occurs either because the subject of the extension is not distinct from the matter introduced by the preceding team or, more commonly, the arguments are distinct but are structured and presented in a way that doesn't highlight the distinction between the opening and closing teams. If the problem is caused by the lack of substantive distinction, the solution is clear: the Member should choose arguments that are more distinct from those of the opening team.

If the problem results from a failure to effectively communicate the uniqueness of the extension, the solution is a bit more nuanced. First, recall my advice above to choose a singular focus for the extension. One clear idea is easier for an adjudicator to distinguish from other teams' arguments than are three or four separate lines of argument. Moreover, extensions should be made explicit in the round. While not required to brand the extension as such by actually saying, "And now I'm going to develop Closing Proposition's extension . . ." savvy debaters will recognize that whatever aesthetic tradeoff is made by doing so the advantage of clarity may well justify the decision. Far more subtle approaches to telling adjudicators that you're transitioning to your extension material are available: after deconstructing the preceding arguments, for example, you may indicate to adjudicators that you're moving on to your extension by saying something as simple as, "Now I would like to address what the Closing Proposition believes is a critical issue that has, until now, been ignored in the debate . . ." Make it a priority to develop a few stock transition phrases that may serve in a variety of rounds and use the structural devices discussed in Chapter 4 to make the extension distinct.

The final potential challenge for a Member speaker establishing an extension is knifing. Drawn from the expression "to stick a knife in the back" of someone, knifing refers to a situation in which a closing team's extension abandons the line of argument adopted by the opening team. Imagine, for example, a debate in which the Opening Proposition argues in favor of banning smoking across the board, making the production, sale, purchase, and possession of cigarettes illegal. If the Closing Proposition, in response to pressure from the Opening Opposition, claims to be responsible just to prove that smoking cigarettes should be banned only in public places (and not, for example, in private domiciles), the Closing Proposition has effectively "knifed" the Opening Proposition. This is a cardinal sin in BP debating; if the adjudicators were to accept this new focus of the round, it would render the first half of the debate largely irrelevant. The most egregious examples of knifing are those motivated by a closing team's desire to circumvent difficult ground defined by the opening teams. A team who commits an obvious knife can expect to be heavily penalized by the adjudicators.

Of course, the other side of the knifing coin is the perennial question of what options exist for a closing team that is cast into a potentially untenable (or at least undesirable) position by an opening team. In short, the general answer is "not many." Even in those cases where the opening team offers an unusual definition of the motion, the closing teams have a responsibility to do their best to support their opening team. Finding a palatable way to argue what may be an unpalatable position is typically evaluated very favorably by adjudicators; some teams actually like their opening teams to place them into extraordinarily difficult situations in the belief the adjudicators are more likely to evaluate the closing team's arguments generously.

In sum, the priority of supporting the opening team should at this point be clear. Regardless of the general approach taken by the extension, you must be sure that the extension's material supports the direction of argument the opening team introduced.

THE MP SPEECH IN THE CAPITAL PUNISHMENT DEBATE

In the capital punishment debate, the Member Proposition (MP) opens her speech with a brief deconstructive effort that both answers the preceding arguments and sets the stage for the extension. With regard to the question of maintaining capital punishment for crimes against humanity, the MP argues that — like with other capital crimes — there will be no deterrent effect for crimes against humanity. Because these crimes are not undertaken in a context where consequences are typically contemplated, she argues, consideration of the action will not produce a reluctance to commit such crimes. On the issue of justice, the MP opts to redirect the discussion to ground that is more in line with the extension she plans to offer: rather than a consideration of whether or not justice is achieved or achievable with the imposition of capital punishment, the MP chooses to question the very notion of justice itself. Perhaps, she argues, justice can't be made manifest until healing occurs. Forgiveness and moving on, not an obsession with vengeance and retribution, are the foundation for justice and, consequently, peace, whether for an individual or a people.

With this foundational work done, the MP moves on to her team's extension. Having seen the Opening Proposition ground their arguments in a decidedly pragmatic analysis of the problems associated with the administration of capital punishment, the MP chooses to focus on the moral objections to capital punishment as the theme of her extension. To support the broad assertion that capital punishment is morally unsustainable, the MP develops two positions.

First, she claims that capital punishment dehumanizes the state that practices it. To reconcile the inconsistency of the prohibition against murder and the practice of capital punishment requires that the citizens view the bureaucracy of the state as separate and distinct from the citizens; it's illegal for a citizen to kill another citizen but it's acceptable for the state to do so. By putting the state in the position of killing its citizens, the practice of capital punishment creates the machinery of the state as something other than human and, consequently, not subject to the same morality as humans. This has the further consequence of making citizens subject to the will of the state, as they perceive the state as something other than (and likely more powerful than) themselves. The implications for legitimizing authoritarian states, claims the MP, are clear.

Additionally, the MP claims that even if capital punishment were only applied to crimes against humanity—arguably the most egregious and clear examples of a crime warranting the death penalty—the state becomes complicit in those crimes. Building on the assertion of the Opening Opposition that we need an unambiguous moral stance with regard to crimes against humanity, the MP argues that practicing capital punishment actually blurs the line by responding to violence and death with more violence and death.

By focusing the bulk of her attention on the development of the morality position, the MP is attempting to capture the attention of the adjudicators and ensure that when the ranking of teams occurs, the Closing Proposition's contribution to the round will be clear.

Recorded in the notes of a round, the MP's speech might look like this:

Prime Minister	Leader Opposition
Model: All UN members cease immediately; convert to life sentences	**Deterrence**? Cannot measure effect **Errors**? In application, not in CP itself; fix system

1. CP doesn't deter crime
    A. No empirical proof
    B. c/n deter crimes of passion
2. Errors irreversible
    A. The system is fallible
	Team Line: Preserve CP for crimes against humanity
	A. Justice demands retribution
	    1. Balance depends on
	    payment of debt
	    2. Provides closure
	B. Need unambiguous moral stance

Deputy Prime Minister	Deputy Leader Opposition
CAH? should prohibit in all cases	**Practical vs. Justice?**
Justice? Exists only with fair application of laws	A. Justice is an ideal; strive even if not perfect
	B. System can be improved; doesn't prove CP unjust
1. Practical concerns prevent justice	
A. No deterrence: no evidence of success	**Justice**
B. Errors rampant, compromise justice	A. Need balance & clarity
C. Racist application	B. CP for CAH = improve the human condition

Member Proposition	Member Opposition
CAH? Will not be deterred	
Justice? Not only about retribution; healing	
1. Moral objections to CP	
A. Killing is killing	
B. CP dehumanizes the state	
C. Complicity in crimes against humanity	

Proposition Whip	Opposition Whip

The MO Speech in the Capital Punishment Debate

Like the MP, the Member Opposition (MO) must also strive to establish a unique argumentative identity in the round. Unlike the MP, the MO will attempt to do so not by focusing on a line of argument not yet contemplated in the round but by offering a case study to prove the proposition untrue.

The MO opens with a deconstructive effort. With regard to the MP's arguments about morality, the MO argues that to not provide the strongest sanction for crimes society deems unconscionable is an immoral act. In an effort to be responsive to the arguments of the Opening Opposition, the MO claims that while healing may be part of justice, the retribution and closure that result from the application of capital punishment — particularly for victims — may also be an important part of their healing.

The MO then turns his attention to a case study. Knowing that he is obligated to defend the stance taken by the Opening Opposition — in this case, to advocate for capital punishment for those who commit crimes against humanity — the MO chooses to explicate the case of one particular suspected war criminal in an effort to demonstrate that the severity of crimes of this nature warrant capital punishment. The case examined by the MO is that of Ratko Mladic, a Serbian military officer who was allegedly involved in a variety of acts classified as war crimes and crimes against humanity during the period of 1992–95 in the Bosnian/Serbian conflict.

On July 24, 1995, the International Criminal Tribunal for the Former Yugoslavia issued an indictment for Mladic; that indictment was amended later in 1995 to include charges of genocide committed at the Srebrenica massacre in July 1995. Mladic's alleged crimes range from ordering sniping campaigns against civilians in Sarajevo to taking UN

Peacekeeping personnel hostage and assisting in the coordination of the Srebrenica massacre, in which over 8,000 Bosniaks were killed by the Serbian military. Mladic has thus far evaded capture and is still at large. If arrested, tried, and convicted of the crimes of which he has been accused, argues the MO, Mladic should be executed. After the MO's speech, the notes of the round might read as follows:

Prime Minister	Leader Opposition
Model: All UN members cease immediately; convert to life sentences	**Deterrence**? Cannot measure effect **Errors**? In application, not in CP itself; fix system

1. CP doesn't deter crime
     A. No empirical proof
     B. c/n deter crimes of passion
 2. Errors irreversible
     A. The system is fallible
	Team Line: Preserve CP for crimes against humanity
	 A. Justice demands retribution
	     1. Balance depends on payment of debt
	     2. Provides closure
	 B. Need unambiguous moral stance

Deputy Prime Minister	Deputy Leader Opposition
CAH? should prohibit in all cases	**Practical vs. Justice?**
Justice? Exists only with fair application of laws	A. Justice is an ideal; strive even if not perfect
	B. System can be improved; doesn't prove CP unjust
1. Practical concerns prevent justice	
A. No deterrence: no evidence of success	**Justice**
B. Errors rampant, compromise justice	A. Need balance & clarity
	B. CP for CAH = improve the human condition
C. Racist application	

Member Proposition	Member Opposition
CAH? Will not be deterred	**Moral**? Immoral to not provide strongest sanction
Justice? Not only about retribution; healing	**Justice**? Retribution, closure can be healing
1. Moral objections to CP	
A. Killing is killing	**Case study**: Ratko Mladic (Serbia)
B. CP dehumanizes the state	A. Complicity in the massacre at Srebrenica in 1995
C. Complicity in crimes against humanity	B. Indictment by Int. Crim. Trib. for Yugoslavia
	C. Mladic still at large, evaded capture and trial

Proposition Whip	Opposition Whip

The Whip Speeches

As the final two speakers in the round, the Whip speakers must balance a responsibility to contribute to their team's effort with a responsibility to summarize the round as it has unfolded. This balancing act can pull a Whip speaker in two directions; an effective Whip must meet both obligations to be successful.

One important note at the outset: there is no "right" way to summarize a round. Some Whip speakers proceed through the round speaker-by-speaker or team-by-team in an effort to recap each argument. While this may be effective for some, it is certainly not required. Other Whip speakers prefer to summarize all the arguments of one side before addressing the arguments of the other side. Again, while some Whips may be adept at this approach, it is not the only way to summarize the round. The approach described below offers yet another way to approach the summary of a BP round. I believe that my approach is quite effective, but you may find your own preferences lead you in a different direction.

CONSTRUCTION AND DECONSTRUCTION

Though primarily summaries, the Whip speeches still maintain a responsibility to engage in both constructive and deconstructive argumentation. As we'll see, this is typically done to frame the round retrospectively. However, there are a several important points about constructive and deconstructive argument worthy of note.

Generally, Whips are prohibited from introducing new lines of argument. Thus, they have little leeway in bringing new constructive material to the round, particularly if that constructive material appears to be substantively different from lines of argument already introduced by their side of the bench. Some exceptions are made for offering new evidence to support an existing line of argument (this is how the Whip speaker satisfies the expectation that he will contribute positive matter to the round), and for the Proposition Whip speaker, deconstruction of the MO's new constructive material (since the PW is the only Proposition speaker with an opportunity to respond to the Closing Opposition's extension).

The PW must understand the strategic approach of the MO, formulate an effective deconstruction of that approach, and integrate the deconstruction of the extension with the broader summary of the round. This, not surprisingly, is one of the most challenging speeches in the round. Many Whip speakers, particularly Proposition Whip speakers, opt to separate the deconstructive effort from the summary, fearing that deconstruction of the Closing Opposition's extension in the context of the broader summary of the round will obscure the Closing Proposition's responses to the MO's new constructive material. I tend to subscribe to this approach, particularly for average Whip speakers. Adjudicators may often miss the deconstructive effort if it is "rolled into" the summary.

On the other hand, the Whip speaker's reconstruction of his team's arguments is perfect material for a summary of the round. Particularly if the Whip speaker engages in a deliberate effort to retrospectively frame the round, the representation (and repair) of arguments belonging to the Whip's side of the debate is done most effectively in the summary.

FRAMING

Here is where the real work of the Whip speaker happens. At this point in the debate, the bulk of the descriptive and relational arguments have been made. The factual basis of the claims has likely been resolved (in the mind of the adjudicators, if not through concession by the opposing teams) and the focus of the debate must shift to the evaluative effort of determining which issues should be prioritized over others. At the conclusion of the round, the adjudication panel retires to deliberate; that deliberation is primarily an exercise in comparing and contrasting the issues in the debate. Savvy Whip speakers will get a jump on this process by outlining and evaluating those issues for the adjudicators.[32]

Retrospective framing uses two basic tactics: the relation of arguments to opposing arguments and the relation of issues to the proposition. Relating arguments to opposing arguments refers to the effort to group individual arguments under broad issue headings. This unification of arguments fixes those competing positions in the mind of the judge and makes obvious the points of stasis at which the arguments meet. Whip speakers should strive to condense the round into two to four main issues under which all relevant arguments may be grouped.

As discussed earlier, this process of organizing competing arguments into issues may start much earlier in the debate, perhaps as early as the first speeches of the round. Many rounds, however, proceed through six speeches without any effort to organize competing arguments into issues. If this is the case, the Whip speakers must draw connections between each side's lines of argument and title those connections to establish the issues that the adjudicators may examine to evaluate the round.

Suppose, for example, you were a Whip speaker for the motion "This house would ban smoking." The Proposition has pursued a variety of arguments about a complete ban on smoking, including prohibiting smoking even in private residences. The Opposition has made arguments about this ban, focused primarily on how the ban would be put into effect. Not only is it impossible to monitor every potential smoker's behavior in his own home, claims the Opposition, but the ban will create a black market for tobacco products.

These arguments, though diverse, could be grouped by a Proposition Whip speaker under the heading "Can a ban be enforced?" Presenting these competing arguments within a discreet issue provides context for the adjudicators to compare the competing factual claims of the Proposition and Opposition. Of course, the Proposition Whip speaker would emphasize the arguments that demonstrate the efficacy of a ban while an Opposition Whip would emphasize the lack of efficacy. Either side, though, may use this issue to organize their conception of the round.

Once the relevant arguments have been organized into two to four main issues, the second tactic of retrospective framing becomes relevant: the Whip speakers must now relate the issues to the proposition. This process attempts to arrange the issues in a hierarchy that establishes the Whip speaker's issues as those most important to resolving the propositional question while downplaying the significance of issues most powerful for the opposing side. Consider again our cigarette debate: one issue — likely most compelling for the Opposition — is the efficacy of a ban. The Opposition will probably be able to convince the adjudication panel that a ban will be minimally effective in stopping smoking. Other arguments organized into other issues, however, may be more compelling for the Proposition's case: an issue concerning the tension between smokers' rights and nonsmokers' health would likely be in play in this debate. The Proposition Whip's job, then, is to convince the adjudication panel that while it may be true that a ban won't necessarily stop every potential smoker from smoking, the impact of smoking on nonsmokers is so significant that there is a moral imperative to at least attempt to protect them from a hazardous substance they don't choose to inhale. Of course, the Opposition Whip will be busy attempting to convince the adjudicators that a principle is not sufficient warrant for prohibiting something if that prohibition cannot be effectively enforced. In both cases, the comparison of these issues relative to the proposition is the focus of the Whip speeches.

In general, the organization of a Whip speech varies round by round. The order in which the issues are addressed in any given Whip speech will depend on which issues emerge in the round and which issues the Whip speaker believes are most compelling for her side; as noted earlier, most effective Whip speeches attempt to encapsulate the round in two to four main issues that serve as a basis of comparison for competing lines of argument. The organization of these issues, too, depends on the strategic considerations of each particular round. The general organizational patterns discussed in Chapter 4 may serve useful prompts for organizing a Whip speech. The most critical issues should come last; the issues that address areas of weakness should be dealt with in the middle of the speech. At times, the organization of the issues will depend on the logical progressivity of the issues. Some issues naturally come before others; in the case of the smoking ban, an adjudicator could likely be convinced that she must resolve whether we *should* attempt to ban smoking (the competing rights issue) before she considers whether we *can* ban smoking (the efficacy issue).

If this organic approach of determining and prioritizing issues is too open-ended and general (particularly for novice debaters), there is a standard approach to a Whip speech that provides more direction. This standard approach utilizes three questions around which to organize the summary of the round:

1. What is required to determine the truth of the motion?
2. How does the other side fail to meet this requirement?
3. How do our efforts meet this requirement?

These three questions serve as prompts to organize the Whip speakers' thinking about the motion. The first, "What is required to determine the truth of the motion?" asks about how the adjudicators should determine whether to adopt or reject the motion. In the case of the smoking ban, the Proposition Whip speaker may respond by identifying first the principle-based standard (Do we have an obligation to act?) and then the practical standard (Can we curtail smoking?). From here, the PW moves to the second point to demonstrate how the Opposition has failed to overturn the moral imperative to act and, though the Opposition may have diminished the efficacy of a ban, has failed to prove that a ban would have no net effect on decreasing smoking. In the third point the PW highlights the arguments the Proposition has made about how the rights of nonsmokers outweigh those of smokers and how a ban would work. This simple generic structure can work very well to provide direction to Whip speakers.

The Whip speaker has a heavy burden: as the final speaker for her side, she has the opportunity to control how the adjudicators will perceive the arguments in the round. This burden can be met with careful attention to how issues are constructed and compared to the proposition.

THE PW SPEECH IN THE CAPITAL PUNISHMENT DEBATE

The Proposition Whip (PW) in the capital punishment round opts to forego a separate effort at deconstruction and instead wraps up his treatment of the Closing Opposition's extension in his summary of the round. Given that the MO utilized a case study to substantiate the Opposition's claim that capital punishment is appropriate for crimes against humanity instead of offering a new line of argument, this is a wise choice for the PW.

The PW outlines three issues that encapsulate the debate as it has occurred. The first issue concerns the nature of justice. Here the PW is meeting his deconstructive obligations to engage the major line of argument pursued by the Opposition teams. By gathering 21 minutes of Opposition argument into a single issue, the PW is attempting to minimize the overall impact of the Opposition's contribution to the round. In a case such as this, where the Opposition's arguments fit will under the broad issue of "justice," this approach is likely the best strategic option for the PW. In other cases, such as those where the Opposition mounts a more diverse attack on the proposition or where the Closing Opposition presents an extension that is substantively different from the lines of argument pursued by the Opening Opposition team, this approach would be risky and ill-advised. In this case, though, the PW is able to remind the adjudicators that the administration of justice requires moral authority on the part of the state and that, particularly in the case of those who have committed atrocities—such as Ratko Mladic—the state loses that authority when it kills.

From here the PW moves on to the final two issues: the practical and moral failings of capital punishment. These two issues are essentially re-statements of the respective positions of the Opening and Closing Proposition teams. Note, though, that the Opening Proposition's arguments are presented first (as the second issue in the speech) and the Closing Proposition's extension is represented as the last issue. Though this is chronologically appropriate given the team's positions in the round, it is also strategically advantageous to the Closing Opposition team.

Recorded in the notes of the round, the PW's speech might look as follows:

Prime Minister	Leader Opposition
Model: All UN members cease immediately; convert to life sentences	**Deterrence**? Cannot measure effect **Errors**? In application, not in CP itself; fix system

1. CP doesn't deter crime
    A. No empirical proof
    B. c/n deter crimes of passion
2. Errors irreversible
    A. The system is fallible
	Team Line: Preserve CP for crimes against humanity
	A. Justice demands retribution
	    1. Balance depends on
	    payment of debt
	    2. Provides closure
	B. Need unambiguous moral stance

Deputy Prime Minister	Deputy Leader Opposition
CAH? should prohibit in all cases	**Practical vs. Justice?**
Justice? Exists only with fair application of laws	A. Justice is an ideal; strive even if not perfect
	B. System can be improved; doesn't prove CP unjust
1. Practical concerns prevent justice	
A. No deterrence: no evidence of success	**Justice**
of success	A. Need balance & clarity
B. Errors rampant,	B. CP for CAH = improve the
compromise justice	human condition
C. Racist application	

Member Proposition	Member Opposition
CAH? Will not be deterred	**Moral?** Immoral to not provide strongest sanction
Justice? Not only about retribution; healing	**Justice**? Retribution, closure can be healing
1. Moral objections to CP	
A. Killing is killing	**Case study**: Ratko Mladic (Serbia)
B. CP dehumanizes the state	A. Complicity in the massacre
C. Complicity in crimes	at Srebrenica in 1995
against humanity	B. Indictment by Int. Crim.
	Trib. for Yugoslavia
	C. Mladic still at large,
	evaded capture and trial

Proposition Whip	Opposition Whip

1. Nature of Justice: need moral authority
 2. Practical Failings
     a. No deterrence
     b. Errors and racism
 3. Moral Failings
     a. Dehumanizing and complicity
     b. Cannot object to what you embrace	

THE OW SPEECH IN THE CAPITAL PUNISHMENT DEBATE

Like the PW, the Opposition Whip (OW) chooses not to separate her deconstructive effort from her summary. Also like the PW, the OW chooses three issues to encapsulate the round. In some cases, Opposition Whip speakers may choose to use the same issues utilized by the Proposition Whip. In cases where those issues have been present, well-defined, and utilized by all the teams throughout the round, this approach can be very effective. In this instance, though, the OW creates issues somewhat different from those of the PW.

First, the OW addresses the question "What is justice?" Here she considers the arguments originally advanced by the Opening Opposition team and in play throughout the round. Justice requires balance and closure, claims the OW, but also presents an imperative beyond simple deterrence of crime. This latter point about the utility of justice is likely in response to the MP's claims that crimes against humanity—like other capital crimes in the status quo—are not likely to be deterred by capital punishment.

From this issue, the OW moves to the question of whether capital punishment may be administered fairly. Note that this condensation of the Proposition's arguments is placed in the middle of the OW's speech; she is seeking to minimize the consideration this issue gets in the adjudicators' evaluation of the round. Regarding the fair administration of capital punishment, the OW reminds the adjudicators that there is a difference between the *punishment* and the *application* of that punishment. The proposition before the house, claims the OW, concerns capital punishment as a penalty for criminal behavior. That the system that applies capital punishment may have shortcomings is not an indictment of capital punishment itself, argues the OW.

Finally, the OW closes with a reconsideration of the appropriateness of capital punishment for crimes against humanity. Reaching back to the Opening Opposition's effort, the OW reiterates the general arguments for sanctioning crimes against humanity with execution: that such crimes shock the conscious and that the death penalty is appropriate for both meeting the needs of the survivors of such atrocities and the larger community of humans that benefits from expunging such negative elements from its rolls. The OW closes the final issue — and the debate proper — with a revisitation of the case of Ratko Mladic, demonstrating how one person may have such a gross impact on humanity that his actions warrant his execution.

Recorded in the flow of the debate, the OW's speech would look like this:

Prime Minister	Leader Opposition
Model: All UN members cease immediately; convert to life sentences	**Deterrence**? Cannot measure effect **Errors**? In application, not in CP itself; fix system

1. CP doesn't deter crime
    A. No empirical proof
    B. c/n deter crimes of passion
2. Errors irreversible
    A. The system is fallible
	Team Line: Preserve CP for crimes against humanity
	A. Justice demands retribution
	    1. Balance depends on
	    payment of debt
	    2. Provides closure
	B. Need unambiguous moral stance

Deputy Prime Minister	Deputy Leader Opposition
CAH? should prohibit in all cases **Justice**? Exists only with fair application of laws	**Practical vs. Justice?** A. Justice is an ideal; strive even if not perfect B. System can be improved; doesn't prove CP unjust

1. Practical concerns prevent justice
    A. No deterrence: no evidence of success
    B. Errors rampant, compromise justice
    C. Racist application
	Justice
	A. Need balance & clarity
	B. CP for CAH = improve the human condition

Member Proposition	Member Opposition
CAH? Will not be deterred	**Moral**? Immoral to not provide
Justice? Not only about	strongest sanction
retribution; healing	**Justice**? Retribution, closure can
	be healing
1. Moral objections to CP	
A. Killing is killing	**Case study**: Ratko Mladic (Serbia)
B. CP dehumanizes the state	A. Complicity in the
C. Complicity in crimes	massacre at Srebrenica in
against humanity	1995
	B. Indictment by Int. Crim.
	Trib. for Yugoslavia
	C. Mladic still at large,
	evaded capture and trial

Proposition Whip	Opposition Whip
1. Nature of Justice: need moral	**A**. What is Justice?
authority	1. Balance and closure
2. Practical Failings	2. Imperative beyond
a. No deterrence	deterrence
b. Errors and racism	**B**. Can CP be administered fairly?
3. Moral Failings	**C.** Do some crimes warrant
a. Dehumanizing and	death?
complicity	1. Generally: CAH shock the
b. Cannot object to what	conscious
you embrace	2. Specifically: Mladic

Through eight speeches and 56 minutes of debate, the debaters have the opportunity to thoroughly interrogate the question posed by the motion given to them. With careful attention to the basic expectations of each speech and speaker, the chances that these questions will be explored appropriately increases markedly.

CHAPTER 6

Decision Making and Strategy

Much of the advice written for debaters is from the perspective of the person undertaking the persuasive effort: the debater. Advice on the proper structuring of arguments, the appropriate evidence to employ, and the correct conduct in the round tends to be presented from a very prescriptive point of view. Do this, the advice seems to imply, and you'll be successful. Indeed, this very book often employs this perspective.

It's curious that more written about debating doesn't place the people most important to the debater's success — the adjudicators — at the forefront of the guidance offered. If most debaters' objective is to win rounds, shouldn't we spend some time discussing how the people ultimately making the decision about who wins and loses actually *make* that decision?

As I'll discuss in this chapter, an understanding of how human beings make decisions is not only advantageous for debaters, it is a prerequisite to effective debating. The study of decision making is quickly becoming recognized as a discreet discipline that, though it has application in nearly every facet of human behavior, shares a common set of principles and practices. In his text, *Thinking and Deciding*, psychologist Jonathan Baron offers a thorough introduction to the study of human thought and decision making. This chapter is largely based on Baron's work.

My goals for this chapter are twofold: first, I intend to examine the process of human thinking and decision making as discussed by Baron. Using this foundation, I'll adapt Baron's work to provide a model for presenting arguments in a way that attempts to parallel the process of decision making employed by the adjudicators.

I believe the latter goal is particularly valuable, as the extemporaneous nature of parliamentary debating means that the debaters argue over, and the adjudicators must make decisions about, a variety of topics throughout the course of a tournament. Because the topics differ round by round, the decision adjudicators make in each round will also differ. Unlike the legal field, where decisions follow well-established patterns involving consideration of the facts, precedent, and law, or the field of medicine, where decisions are guided by protocols designed to balance aggressive treatment of disease against risk to the patient, the practice of decision making in competitive parliamentary debating doesn't occur in a context defined by consistent subject matter in which a standardized approach to decision making may develop.

In the course of any given parliamentary debating tournament, topics may range from international relations to biomedical issues to energy policy to the state's role in interpersonal relationships. Clearly, identifying a method of decision making useful in all these cases is challenging. Even those critical models that have proved useful for competitive debating — such as the stock issues model prevalent in competitive policy debating in the United States — are less practical when the topics in competitive parliamentary debating may range from a consideration of what something is ("Iran's Revolutionary Guard is a terrorist organization") to the relationship between things ("Consumption of violent media increases the tendency for violent behavior") to preferred courses of action ("Smoking in public should be banned"). In each of these cases, the approach to decision making will be different; any model must be flexible enough to be useful in all of these cases.

I begin with the assumption that the practice of debating is, when reduced to its essence, and exercise in decision making. Those charged with making the decision — the adjudicators — are responsible for listening to the positions and perspectives of each team to determine whether they believe the motion to be true or false. For an adjudicator to reach this decision requires that she progress through the same general process she would employ to decide whether or not to attend the debating tournament in the first place or to wear a sweater to the tournament or to make any other decision in her life. The decision-making process, as I'll discuss below, is relatively consistent and predictable regardless of the nature of the decision being made.

Insight into this process is valuable to debaters. Put simply, understanding how adjudicators *think* is perhaps the most valuable asset a debater may possess. Knowing this allows the debater to present information of a nature and in an order that parallels the way in which adjudicators make their decisions. This chapter offers a brief introduction to the process of thinking and deciding; the chapter on adjudication offers a more focused consideration of how adjudicators of British Parliamentary academic debating contests think.

The Nature of Thinking and Deciding

Early in his book, Baron makes clear the goal of his writing: to promote rational thinking.[33] In general, *thinking* is that fundamentally human activity in which we engage whenever we encounter uncertainty:

> We think when we are in doubt about how to act, what to believe or what to desire. In these situations, thinking helps us to resolve our doubts: It is purposive.[34]

According to Baron, *rational* thinking is that which helps people achieve their goals. *Rationality* for Baron—unlike popular misconceptions of the term—is not logical thought exclusive of emotional influence. Rather, rational thinking is characterized by awareness of the goals we seek, the possibilities we have before us to meet those goals, and the evidence of the desirability of each of those possibilities relative to our goals.

Decision making employs a two-step process Baron calls the *search-inference framework*. According to Baron, making a decision involves the *search* for the relevant elements required to make the decision and, once those elements are discovered, the *inference* from the known (the elements discovered) to the unknown (the best decision).

Baron characterizes the search portion of the search-inference framework as an exploration. Reacting to a certain motivation (uncertainty about what to do next, for example), a person seeks to discover those elements required to make the decision that will satisfy the motive. These elements include the *possibilities* (the options from which the decision maker may select), the *goals* (the outcomes or end states desired by the individual making the decision), and the *evidence* (the data relevant to demonstrating the desirability of each possibility). Each of these elements will be discussed in more detail later in the chapter and will serve as the foundation for the decision-making model drawn from Baron's work.

The *search* for those elements in individual decision making proceeds from two general starting points: we may recall these elements from our own experience and our search for these elements may be influenced by external sources.[35] In terms useful to academic debating, we could say that the decision-making process through which the adjudicators proceed is initiated by the presentation of a controversial proposition; that proposition creates uncertainty in the adjudicators' mind about its truth or falsity. From there, the search phase of the decision-making process requires the exploration of elements relevant to resolving that proposition. This exploration is influenced both by recall (the adjudicators' knowledge, perceptions, and beliefs relative to the proposition) and external sources (the efforts to the debaters to present the adjudicators with possibilities, goals, and evidence relevant to their decisions). The challenge to debaters, at least for the search portion of the decision-making process, is to help the adjudicators explore the decision in a way that is sensitive to the information they already possess and present them with other, relevant information useful in making their decision.

The second step of the search-inference framework involves the assessment of the elements discovered to determine the best outcome. As noted above, this stage of decision making is *inferential* because it involves a move from the known (those elements discovered) to the unknown (the best decision). In terms of academic debating, this is the process that occurs when the adjudicators contemplate and reach their decision. That is not to say that the inferential process occurs only after the round and, as such, is not subject to the debaters' influence. Though many debates seem to end with the debaters satisfied with presenting only those elements adjudicators require to make their decisions, successful debaters know that the inferential process is equally subject to their persuasive efforts. Influencing which goals adjudicators will seek to satisfy (and in which order), which evidence the adjudicators find most compelling, and, therefore, which possibility the adjudicators prefer is arguably the most important strategic effort a debater may undertake.

This discussion of the search-inference framework thus far gives the appearance that decision making is an orderly, logically progressive exercise. Baron makes clear that this is not the case:

> The processes of thinking—the search for possibilities, evidence, and goals and the use of the evidence to evaluate possibilities— do not occur in any fixed order. They overlap. The thinker alternates from one to another.[36]

Rational thinking demands a disorganized, nonsequential approach: to be open to options, alterations, and arguments as thinking progresses is to seek the best decision. It is convenient, however, to separate these two stages for the purpose of elaborating and adapting each to the purposes of academic debating.

Uncovering the Elements of Decision Making: The "Search"

Decision making begins with some prompt; Baron refers to this motivation as "doubt."[37] In our lives, we may have doubt about which product we should buy, where we should attend college, or what we should eat for lunch. In an academic debate, the proposition is the prompt for decision making: the controversial nature of the proposition creates doubt about its truth or falsity. Debating, then, may be seen as an effort on the part of the participants to influence the adjudicators' effort to resolve this doubt.

As noted above, the first step toward resolving doubt is the exploration of the elements required to make the decision: those elements include possibilities, goals, and evidence.

POSSIBILITIES

Possibilities are the available means of resolving doubt. In debate terms, the possibilities are options from which the adjudicators may choose. At their most simple, the possibilities available to adjudicators may be seen as either the affirmation or the negation of the motion as presented. If the motion is "Capital punishment should be banned," the possibilities available to the adjudicators seem to be (1) banning capital punishment or (2) not banning capital punishment.

The creation of possibilities, though, goes beyond these simple binary alternatives presented by the motion. Remember that the proposition, not the motion, defines the locus of conflict between the teams in the round. In other words, though the motion presented to the debaters influences and informs the debate in which they'll participate, the proposition is the point of stasis around which their arguments coalesce. This point of stasis is the product of the debater's arguments.

A debater's early strategic priority must be to control the possibilities available to adjudicators. For the Proposition teams, this typically is done through their interpretation of the motion. Refer to the debate on capital punishment discussed in the preceding chapter: though the motion was "Capital punishment should be banned," the PM had at his disposal a variety of options, each of which would have created a different set of possibilities for the adjudicators: he could have argued, for example, to ban capital punishment for minors; he could have presented a case arguing for an end to capital punishment for certain crimes; or, as he did in our example, he could have opted to argue for an end to capital punishment for all crimes in all cases. Any of these options would have presented a different possibility for the adjudicators to evaluate.[38] Typically, the Opening Proposition team presents the *possibility* they'll defend as their *model*.

Opposition teams also benefit from developing an explicit possibility in the round. Of course, the *de facto* possibility represented by Opposition teams is "*not* whatever the Proposition proposes," but a more considered approach to affiliating with a possibility may have strategic advantage for an Opposition team.

Opposition teams may present a variety of alternative possibilities: they may invest themselves in a particular team line (such as advocating capital punishment be preserved for crimes against humanity, as did the Opposition team in the example round in Chapter 5); they may offer a countermodel that seeks to solve the problem(s) outlined by the Proposition in a way that is mutually exclusive with and preferable to the model advocated by the Proposition; or they may advocate that the status quo is a possibility preferable to what the Proposition advocates. Each of these possibilities (and this is by no means an exhaustive list) has certain advantages and disadvantages, but each shares the common characteristic of offering a positive option as that team's possibility rather than a default alternative. An possibility that you control is preferable to a *de facto* alternative or one imposed by the adjudicators or the opposing team.

All possibilities, according to Baron, have *strength value* relative to the goals sought by the decision maker. The strength of any particular possibility is influenced by the evidence (either positive or negative evidence) offered on that possibility's behalf. A decision is reached by evaluating this evidence to determine the strength of the possibility relative to the goals sought. In a debate round, the adjudicators' decision will be based on their perception of the strength of each possibility relative to the goal(s) sought.

GOALS

Once the possibilities have been discovered, the evaluation of those possibilities requires some standard against which those possibilities may be evaluated. *Goals* are the standards by which decision makers evaluate possibilities. Imagine trying to reach a decision about which new car to buy: the various models available (the *possibilities*) are evaluated according to the *goals* you seek; those goals may include concerns such as performance, affordability, safety, reliability, and appearance. The application of these goals to the possibilities will produce a decision.

Goals are not objective, absolute phenomena that preexist our decision making. In fact, as is implied in their inclusion in the *search* portion of the search-inference framework, goals themselves are varied, malleable, and relative to each decision we make. This may be seen in an extension of the above example; if you and I both need to decide on a new automobile, it's very likely that we'll reach different conclusions about which car is best. I may apply safety, reliability, and affordability as my goals while you may opt to choose a car with outstanding performance and appearance. Clearly, we may differ in our goals and, as a result, we'll select different possibilities.

We can also recognize that the goals we utilize are closely tied to the values we possess. The desired outcomes of our decision making are tangible expressions of our values: we value our health and well-being, so we set as a goal the safety of our car. We value our image and reputation, so we set as a goal owning an attractive automobile. This connection between values and goals is critical to understanding how goals operate in decision making.

There are two explanations why we may arrive at different conclusions for the same decision. First, we may be using different *goals sys-*

tems. A goals system is a defined group of goals. A system of goals may be defined in a variety of ways: goals may be standardized for a particular context (often, literature advising consumers how to select their new car will index the potential goals that may be relevant to their decision), by a field of decision making (such as the examples of law and medicine discussed above), by a culture (consider the difference between Western and Eastern values and how those differences influence the outcome of decisions, for example), or by nearly any other factor that may be used to define a group of people and the things they value (such as gender, ethnicity, ideology, geography, etc.). But even these systems are not fixed; what one person who belongs to a particular group may define as the system of goals for that group may be quite different from those values defined by other members of that same group (think about the diversity of goals pursued by those who affiliate with the Democratic Party in the United States, for example).

For debaters, goals systems are useful as prompts: they remind us of the goals that may be relevant to any particular decision. Savvy debaters will design a strategy and choose possibilities that correspond to the system of goals relevant to their decision.

The second explanation for why you and I may reach a different conclusion for the same decision is that, while we may share the same goals within a particular system, we prioritize those goals differently. This is the more likely explanation for our choice of different cars: we don't possess different goals systems; we merely differ on how the goals within that system should be prioritized. It's unlikely that you're unconcerned with the affordability, economy, or reliability of your new car; you simply choose to prioritize performance and appearance above those other goals. The ordering of goals within a goals system produces a *goals hierarchy*.

For our car decision, our respective goals hierarchies might look like this:

Your Goals Hierarchy

Appearance

Performance

Reliability

Affordability

Safety

My Goals Hierarchy

Safety

Reliability

Affordability

Appearance

Performance

Though we're operating with the same system of goals, how we prioritize those goals within that system differs. Our different goal hierarchies will result in different decisions. In the context of a debate, adjudicators often are asked to choose between two competing goals hierarchies to reach their decision about which possibility they prefer.

Debaters must control the system and hierarchy of the goals the adjudicators will use. This starts with a realistic acknowledgment of the goals system relevant to the motion. Often, debaters mistakenly ignore the goals of their opponents, deny that their opponents' goals are legitimate (or relevant), or attempt to limit the decision-making criteria to a single goal. Any of these approaches is a mistake, as each leads to artificial and truncated (Baron would say *irrational*) decision making.

Imagine the capital punishment debate if one team convinced the adjudicators that the only goal relevant to their decision was the pursuit of justice. Such a debate would ignore the moral, economic, practical, and other goals that may be critical to making the decision. A more rational approach is to acknowledge the presence of those other goals in the decision's goals system, but to then present arguments about why the goal of justice should be placed at the top of the goals hierarchy for this particular decision.

I'll discuss how you can prioritize goals into a coherent goals hierarchy below.

EVIDENCE

Evidence is data that affects the strength of any possibility relative to a goal. According to Baron:

> Evidence can consist of simple propositions . . . or it can consist of arguments, imagined scenarios, or examples. One possibility can serve as evidence against another as when we challenge a scientific hypothesis by giving an alternative and incompatible explanation of the data.[39]

Evidence, as a decision maker considers it, is proof of the ability (or inability) of a possibility to meet a goal. In my car decision, the evidence I consider to evaluate the possibilities against my goals may include data such as fuel economy, cost, available body styles and colors, crash performance, and so forth.

Decision-makers evaluate evidence by according it *weight*: the more relevant a particular piece of evidence is to whether a possibility meets a particular goal, the greater weight that evidence is accorded. If my paramount goal in the car decision is safety, I will give the most weight to evidence of the cars ability to keep me (and my passengers) safe. For me, how quickly the cars accelerate would be accorded less weight, given the low position of performance in my goal hierarchy.

Evidence may also be either positive or negative relative to a particular goal. The same piece of data—the weight of the car I'm considering, for example—may be either positive or negative according to my goals. If I'm concerned about safety, I may believe that a large, heavy car offers more protection in a collision. If, on the other hand, I'm most concerned with performance, that a particular car is heavy would likely be perceived negatively.

Debaters must generate, organize, and present compelling evidence on behalf of their possibility. The evidence may be factual, drawn from qualitative or quantitative representations of data more commonly known (respectively) as examples or statistics, or it may take the form of argument: theories, values, and beliefs are types of evidence that require logical substantiation to be convincing. Regardless of the situation, winning debaters will be adept at choosing and utilizing the evidence most likely to convince the adjudicators of the strength of their preferred possibility.

Evaluating the Elements of Decision Making: The "Inference"

The search for the elements relevant to the decision naturally leads to the inferential phase: reaching a decision requires that the decision maker prioritize the various goals desired and, once a goals hierarchy is established, choose from among the possibilities available. While this chapter discusses those phases as separate processes, as Baron notes, the inferential process tends to parallel the search process. In informal decision making, elements are evaluated as they are discovered. Moreover, Baron recognizes the interconnectedness of the elements of the decision: evidence affects the strength of possibilities; goals affect the weight accorded to evidence. Debaters can benefit, however, from delineating and structuring this process in an effort to guide the adjudicators' decision.

In a structured decision-making process, the logical progression is from discovery of goals to the creation of a goals hierarchy, then from the discovery of possibilities to the selection of the best possibility. Rational decision making depends on a thorough understanding of the outcomes sought before the possibilities for accomplishing those outcomes may be evaluated. In like fashion, this section will discuss first the organization of goals into a goals hierarchy and then the evaluation of the possibilities according to the goals. This approach is not to imply that early speakers or teams focus on one part of the process and latter speakers and teams focus on the other part; winning debaters will recognize that regardless of which of the speaking positions they occupy, they benefit from simultaneously guiding the adjudicators' search for the elements relevant to the decision and the adjudicators' evaluation of those elements.

IDENTIFYING THE PREFERRED GOALS HIERARCHY

Though a system of goals may be defined by a variety of factors, in practice, the system of goals in play in a debate round is defined by those goals the debaters seek.[40] The goals may be explicitly identified or, more typically, may be the product of the arguments the debaters make. In a debate about banning tobacco, for example, the Proposition may make arguments not only about the health consequences of second-hand smoke and the attendant financial costs but about the right of nonsmokers to avoid smoke, the special consideration that must be accorded to the health of children of smokers and the imperative to protect people from the corporations willing to exploit the addictive properties of their products to insure their profitability. From these arguments, we may identify the Proposition's preferred goals as (1) saving money, (2) protecting the freedom of choice, (3) shielding children from harm, and (4) defending consumers from predatory corporate practices.

On the other hand, the Opposition may argue that while a ban on smoking in those situations where those who choose not (or cannot choose) to smoke is warranted, tobacco should not be banned totally. Such a team line may be supported by arguments claiming that the tobacco industry is an important part of our economy, that smokers have a right to choose to smoke and that only such a partial ban can be enforced successfully. From the Opposition's position, we can gather that they're concerned with two of the goals advocated by the Proposition — protecting individual rights to choose and saving money — and one new goal not mentioned by the Proposition: creating an efficacious policy. Represented holistically, the system of goals in operation for the decision to be made in this round might look like this:

Guiding the adjudicators' decision requires that the debaters establish a particular goals hierarchy from the system of goals relevant to the proposition for their debate. Early in their speeches, debaters must make an important strategic decision: should they adopt the hierarchy advocated by their opponents or should they attempt to establish their own, alternate goals hierarchy?

The former strategy is preferable if the debaters believe that they can convince the adjudicators that their possibility meets the goals their opponents embrace better than their opponents' possibility. Put simply, it's easier to win by endorsing ground claimed by your opponents (their goals hierarchy) and then defeating them on that ground by proving your possibility better meets those goals.

Consider our tobacco debate. The Proposition team built a case arguing (at least in part) that second-hand smoke creates health consequences that are costly, not only to the individual affected but to the society as a whole in the form of increased public health expenses, increased insurance rates, etc. Rather than attempting to counter the Proposition by arguing that such costs are negligible or that the financial savings are outweighed by the detriment to individual rights, an Opposition team may argue that the actual financial benefits of a ban on tobacco might be outweighed by the costs of policing that ban: enforcing a prohibition on tobacco would create monitoring, investigation, interdiction, prosecution, and incarceration expenses that currently don't exist. If the Proposition has convinced the adjudicator to be concerned with cost savings, an Opposition team may argue, they are better off *not* banning tobacco sales. This strategy is particularly effective because — assuming that the Opposition can substantiate their claims about the increased policing costs — the Proposition can hardly object that such expenses aren't relevant to the decision given that it was the Proposition team who introduced the goal of saving money in the first place.

Unfortunately, such direct comparisons are relatively rare. More common is for debaters to argue that the goals *they* pursue are more important than the goals advocated by their opponents. The ranking of goals in a hierarchy requires that debaters identify the system of goals in operation in the round and present arguments about why the goals they favor should be ranked above those of their opponents.

The system for the tobacco round is a set of goals relevant to the decision to be made; the clash in the debate will likely be over the prioritization of goals in that system. The Proposition, recognizing both the sympathetic potency of some of their goals (particularly the innocent children who can't choose not to smoke if their parents do) and that one of their goals isn't shared by the Opposition (defending consumers), will likely seek to convince the adjudicators that those are the most critical goals in the round. The Opposition, on the other hand, may seek to place at the top of their hierarchy the goals of protecting freedom of choice, avoiding economic costs, and the efficacy of the policy.

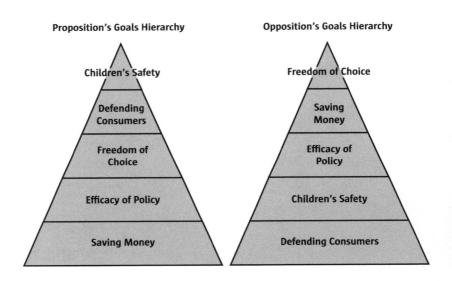

Thus, the struggle in this round is for each side to convince the adjudicators that their hierarchy is the appropriate ranking of goals with which the decision should be made. The claim that your goals are more important than your opponents may be substantiated in a variety of ways:

Scope of goals: Some goals may be argued to be preferable because they subsume others. A concern for fuel economy when making a car decision, for example, may be subsumed by the larger goal of affordability: if a purchaser seeks to save money on fuel but ignores the overall costs of the car (including the purchase price, the licensing and registration fees, the tax, and the financing costs, for example), he may end up spending more to purchase the car than he saves in fuel costs. The broader goal would therefore be ranked higher in this consideration.[41]

Context-specific goals: Some goals are more important than others given the context of the decision. Imagine, for example, a conflict in which an individual files a bogus lawsuit against a corporation claiming some harm and demanding compensation. The corporate executives, recognizing the ridiculousness of the claim, know that if they proceed to litigation they will likely be exonerated of any responsibility. Nonetheless, they may choose to settle the claim before the case is tried. Why? Because in their preferred context, such a decision represents the best possibility to meet their goal. In a legal context, the goal is the pursuit of truth: "did the injury occur and, if so, what is appropriate compensation?" is the only concern of the court. If this were the concern of the corporation, the best choice would be to proceed to litigation, where the corporation would likely prevail. From a business perspective, however, where the ultimate goal is profitability, it may be worth settling such a case to avoid the time and expense of litigating. The context in which the decision is made affects the prioritization of the relevant goals.

Exclusive or contradictory goals: A strong case can be made for preferring goals that don't exclude or contradict other goals. Given the complexity and interrelatedness of goals pursued in decision making, those goals that exclude others should be assessed with particular scrutiny. For example, those who argue against the expansion of oil exploration and development in wilderness areas often claim that any such development compromises the wild nature of the area and must be prohibited. These advocates' goal of preserving the environment is, in this case, absolutely exclusive with their opponents' goal of economic development. The hegemony of a single goal, claim those in favor of development, is inherently unfair given its exclusion of a goal legitimately held by others with a stake in the decision.

Terminal and instrumental goals: Earlier I made the connection between goals and the values we possess. In his work on human values, social psychologist Milton Rokeach distinguished between terminal and instrumental values.[42] Terminal values are those that have inherent value; instrumental values are prized because they facilitate our pursuit of terminal values. This distinction may also be useful to distinguish between the goals sought in a decision: those goals that are deemed to be instrumental may be ranked below those that are terminal, particularly if the instrumental goal leads to that particular terminal goal. Consider the question of protecting freedom of speech: many regard freedom of speech not as an end in itself but as facilitative to the larger goal of establishing democracy. In cases where these values are in conflict — such as those cases where particularly offensive speech may marginalize those targeted and disenfranchise them from the democratic process, for example — the goal deemed instrumental (protecting freedom of speech) may be argued to be less important than the terminal goal (democracy).

Qualitative significance: The nature of a particular goal may be argued to be qualitatively more significant than that of other goals. Pursuit of justice, for example, is almost universally held to be more important than the cost of that pursuit. Those goals with greater qualitative significance are arguably more important than those of lesser qualitative significance.

Quantitative significance: Some goals may be argued to be more important because they affect more people. The debate over extending access to the legal institution of marriage to homosexuals in the United States presented an example of this comparative technique. Those who claimed that allowing homosexuals to wed would threaten the institution of marriage sometimes argued that because homosexuals comprised less than 10% of the population, offering them equal access to marriage was less important than protecting the sanctity of marriage for the remainder of the (presumably heterosexual, marriage-inclined) population. In other words, because more people are affected by our goal, their goal is less important. This argument may be made with varying degrees of success.

The goals hierarchy frames the decision faced by the adjudicators: to select from the possibilities represented by the Proposition and Opposition, the adjudicators must arrive first at a ranking of the goals to be achieved. From this effort, the adjudicators then proceed to evaluate the strength of the possibilities relative to the goals sought.

EVALUATING THE STRENGTH OF POSSIBILITIES

In some cases, the resolution of the goals hierarchy issue will almost automatically resolve the issue of which possibility the adjudicators prefer. If in the "explore for oil in wilderness areas" debate, for example, the adjudicators are convinced that the goal of preserving wilderness as untrammeled, wild areas is paramount, then the selection of the possibility is clear: the adjudicators will prefer the possibility that prevents oil extraction in these areas. Of course, this simplicity is deceptive. With four competing teams and eight different speeches, not to mention (typically) at least three adjudicators and no on-going feedback during the round as to which goals the adjudicators prefer, identifying the adjudicators' "preferred goals" is at best an inexact science.

Advocating for a particular possibility as the best option is similarly inexact. Put simply, to convince adjudicators that the possibility you represent is the preferable choice, you must convince them that your possibility better corresponds to their preferred goals.

Arguing that your possibility better meets the adjudicator's goals is a process that must be specific to the subject matter of each round. Arguing for the virtues of oil exploration requires different arguments than arguing against a ban on tobacco. Nonetheless, some common approaches can help to prove that your possibility is preferable:

Argue that your possibility best corresponds with the preferred goal hierarchy. The most basic approach to proving that your possibility is preferable is to offer compelling evidence on behalf of your possibility. Remember that evidence—as one of Baron's elements of decision making—may be comprised of fact or argument. The adjudicator's preference for your possibility depends on the quality of evidence you offer of your possibility's capacity to meet the preferred goal(s). Thus, at its core, arguing on behalf of your possibility is an exercise in constructing well-supported, sound, well-structured, and well-presented arguments and, perhaps equally important, proving that your opponents have failed to do the same.

Demonstrate that your possibility meets multiple (more) goals. As noted earlier, adjudicators do not have the opportunity to reveal their developing preferences as the round progresses; debaters won't know until the oral adjudication which goals hierarchy the adjudicators prefer. Moreover, the adjudicators may be convinced that many goals are material to their decision; some of those goals may be the "property" of the Proposition teams, others may belong to the Opposition. One powerful strategy is to demonstrate how your possibility satisfies multiple goals or more goals than the possibility addressed by your opponents. Operating on the premise that all goals are valuable, those possibilities that meet the most goals are typically preferable to those that meet fewer.

Prove that your possibility best balances the tension between goals. All goals, to the extent that they are valued by stakeholders in the conflict, are relevant. A powerful strategy for demonstrating the desirability of your possibility is to argue that your possibility best balances the tension between the equally important goals of all stakeholders in the conflict. The oil exploration debate referenced above presents a good example of this strategy: where one side's possibility (no development) necessarily excludes the opposing possibility, those in favor of development may argue that development can be done in a way that is environmentally sensitive and responsible, thus satisfying both the goals of protecting the environment and promoting economic development.

Positive and negative evidence. As noted earlier, Baron distinguishes between positive evidence (that evidence that demonstrates your possibility meets a goal) and negative evidence (that evidence that demonstrates that a possibility fails to meet a goal). An important strategic decision debaters face is balancing their focus on positive evidence on behalf of their own possibility with offering negative evidence of the relationship between their opponents' possibility and the preferred goals. In general, you should seek to balance your focus on these two strategies; this balance is essentially the same balance sought between constructive argumentation and deconstructive argumentation discussed in Chapter 4.

A more nuanced version of this dilemma lies in the question of how to address your opponents' possibility. Again, two options exist: either you can critique the positive evidence your opponent offered of the relationship between their possibility and the preferred goal, or you may offer your own, negative evidence of the failure of their possibility to meet the goals sought. The risk of the former approach is that even if you diminish the adjudicators' certainty about the ability of your opponents' possibility to meet a goal, you will likely never eliminate it.

Take the smoking ban debate, for example: the side opposed to a ban on smoking may argue that smokers will find ways to circumvent the ban, thus diminishing the likelihood that the ban (the possibility) will curb smoking (the goal). Even in this case, however, the adjudicators may remain convinced that *some* decrease in smoking is likely, even if that decrease is not 100%. For this reason, you should go beyond the mere mitigation of the strength of your opponents' possibility and demonstrate, with negative evidence, the undesirable relationship between the opponents' possibility and the goals sought. You should then compare the diminished strength of your opponents' possibility and the evidence of undesirable relationships between their possibility and goals sought with the evidence of the strength of your possibility relative to the goals.

Offer comparison of possibilities on like terms: Often, quite different possibilities may be compared by assessing the competing options on some common ground. Sometimes, this is obvious: competing possibilities are often proposed to accomplish the same goal. Consider the debate about the U.S. occupation of Iraq. When discussing whether to withdraw troops from Iraq or to continue the occupation, the discussion is often focused on which option best provides for the security of the United States. Both sides seek the paramount goal of national security yet present competing proposals (possibilities) for accomplishing that goal.

Other decisions, though, require modification of terms to compare the possibilities on like grounds. Consider the example of debates over whether to invest public money in safety precautions. There are many ways we could make ourselves safer if we were willing to spend the money to do so. Automobile travel, for example, would be significantly safer if all roads had separate, divided lanes for different traffic directions. Most societies have determined, however, that the value of the lives saved is not worth the amount of money that would be required to convert roads to divided lanes. In this instance, the worth of human life is expressed as financial value that may be compared with the cost of remodeling a road. This approach, while certainly likely to ignore the whole value of a human life, allows a common basis on which competing possibilities may be assessed.

These basic strategies are a starting point for proving that one possibility is preferable to another. Many other approaches—most of which are specific to decision being made—are available to debaters.

By making explicit the process by which a decision may be reached, successful debaters lead their adjudicators through the decision-making process to the conclusion they desire. Even in those rounds where this process is not made particularly explicit by the debaters, knowledge of and attention to the basic assumptions of rational decision making will help you make arguments that are more easily followed, more clearly undersold and, ultimately, more competitively successful than those of their opponents.

CHAPTER 7

The Paradoxes of Debating

The average debating tournament held in the WUDC format features five or six preliminary rounds followed by two to four elimination rounds. The number of teams entered in a particular tournament varies widely, from 16 to 20 at a small intervarsity tournament to over 400 teams at the World Universities Debating Championships. Nearly every weekend during the academic year a tournament is held somewhere; often multiple tournaments are hosted on the same weekend in various locations around the world. In other words, there's a lot of debating going on.

While this is great news for proponents of the powerful skills debating teaches, it poses a significant challenge to those who would advise others on how to win debates—yours truly included. Given the remarkable number of rounds that happen in a competitive season, and given that each round in the WUDC format focuses on a different topic, there's no way to anticipate every possible contingency that may arise in a debate. Winning debaters recognize that to be successful they must be equipped with a variety of tactical options from which they may choose. Those same debaters must also remain flexible enough to adapt their tactics to the demands of a particular round.

In other words, no advice for debating can claim to be inclusive, universal, or applicable in every round.

Instead of attempting to catalog and discuss every tactic available (though I do recommend some specific tactics in the next chapter), I'm taking a different approach. I believe that if debaters are familiar with a set of guiding principles that often leads to success, they can apply those principles to particular situations as they arise. Phrased as paradoxes, these observations suggest a number of starting points from which you can make the best strategic and tactical choices in any particular round.

That these observations are phrased as paradoxes is not a mere coincidence. It is in the tension between what we believe to be correct and the opposite of what we believe to be correct that genuine truth often lies. In other words, what seems to be the conventional wisdom in any given situation is often neither conventional nor wise. These paradoxes are best thought of not as directives but as prompts for your own consideration of the most effective approach to debating.

In the Zen Buddhist tradition, *koans* help to inspire and focus contemplative thought.[43] The most famous koan — what is the sound of one hand clapping? — is typical of these short proverbs designed to provide insight into the nature of the world. By contemplating what appears to be a contradictory statement, students of Zen reflect upon the meaning and method of enlightenment. While I don't claim to offer insight into the eternal, it is in the spirit of enlightened inquiry that I offer these paradoxes. By challenging what we think we know about debating, we can discover something far more important: what we didn't yet know.

Paradox #1: The Quality of a Debate Depends More on Agreement Than Disagreement

Debaters (and nondebaters, for that matter) often imagine good debating as an exclusively contrary exercise where the teams vigorously and vehemently disagree with one another. While certainly disagreement is a prerequisite for debating, the most critical element of an out-standing debate is agreement.

As discussed in Chapter 3, the starting point of any debate is the proposition. The proposition functions as a dividing line between the ground for which those on the Proposition and those on the Opposition are responsible. For a proposition to be effective the teams must agree on that proposition. Those rounds in which the teams disagree about (or uncertain of) the proposition are often difficult to watch, with teams making arguments about different positions that are largely irrelevant to one another. Moreover, in high-quality debates, teams will likely agree not only on the proposition under consideration but also on the issues being debated in the round. The best debates are those in which the arguments of the Proposition and the Opposition revolve around clearly defined points of stasis relevant to the larger question posed by the proposition.

But agreement in a round is about more than agreeing with the other team on that with which you'll disagree. Opposition teams will often find their strategy empowered by agreeing with the Proposition's goal. Few tactics are more effective than agreeing with your opponent's goal and then demonstrating how they fail to meet that goal while you do.[44] Any speaker may find it useful to agree to an opponent's struc-ture and ordering of arguments in order to enhance the clarity of her own deconstructive effort. Successful debaters often find that they may agree with their opponents' evidence but draw a different conclusion from it.

Finally, agreement may come in the form of concessions in the de-bate. Successful debaters are those who recognize the difference in importance among arguments. In a timed event, where you have to make critical decisions about where to direct your argumentative focus, choosing the most important arguments with which to disagree—and identifying those arguments you may concede—is an important skill. Concession may either be tacit—you merely ignore an argument—or it may be explicit, where acknowledging the validity of an opponent's argument allows you to nullify the impact of that argument. In fact, as a former debater once recognized, in BP debating, sometimes the worst thing that can happen to one of your constructive positions is that your opponents ignore it. When that happens—and when the disregard for that argument is based on recognition of that argument's relative unimportance in the round—the consequence is that your argument "drops out of the round" and with it goes your chance of winning the debate. In debating, and particularly in BP debating, winning is not about prevailing on every argument, but the right arguments.

Paradox #2: Winning Arguments Benefit More from Simplicity Than Complexity

BP debates, with four teams and eight debaters attempting to move the adjudicators in different directions, are complex communicative events. For your arguments to occupy space in the adjudicators' minds, they must not only be relevant to their consideration but also be structured in a way that most effectively captures, holds, and defends the ground on which they rest.

Add to that complexity the recognition that the mode of communication employed in a debate round—public speaking—is transitory, and you face an additional burden. Unlike written communication, in which an audience may immediately review material they don't com-

prehend, and unlike conversation, in which the participants may interact to clarify communication they don't understand, debating relies on
a form of communication that is largely unidirectional: from debater to
audience with no "text" to which to refer and limited opportunity for
interaction between the participants. In such a context, clarity of communication is even more important.

Unfortunately, many debaters believe that complex messages win
debates. Seeking to demonstrate their mastery of a subject and their
command of information relevant to the issues being debated, they attempt to construct intricate, nuanced arguments that overwhelm their
opponents with their density. Without a simple structure and strategy
underlying this complexity, such an approach often fails.

The most effective debaters recognize that simplicity is critical to
effectively communicating a message in a public speaking setting. Simplicity refers, in part, to the structure and organization of a message:
the use of structural devices such as previews, transitions, reviews, and
redundancy is critical to creating a message that "sticks" with adjudicators. But the principle of simplicity also applies to the general strategy
pursued by debaters. When faced with the choice of a simple but traditional approach or a novel but complex approach, choose the simple. Adjudicators are more likely to understand and retain such an approach.

Paradox #3: You're More Likely to Persuade an Audience by Focusing on What They Believe Than What They Don't Believe

We create arguments to move our audience; the assumption with
which we often start is that the goal of an argument—that claim we

want our audience to accept — should be our focus. While certainly you have the responsibility of convincing your adjudicators of the claims you make, doing so may be much easier if you begin your preparation by asking what your audience believes rather than focusing on what they don't believe.

From Chapter 2 we know that arguments function by connecting those ideas that our audiences don't yet accept (the claim) to those ideas that they do believe (the support). In much the same way that this principle operates on the microscopic scale for individual arguments, the same principle can function for your overall strategy.

Begin your preparation of a constructive position by asking, "What about the position does my audience already likely believe?" Do they accept that a problem exists and that some solution is required? Do they believe that any particular principle informs the controversy at hand? Do they believe that one approach (offering incentives, for example) is preferable to another (such as threatening sanctions)? From this starting point, you can begin to frame your general strategy.

Further, the concept of presumption in argumentation reveals that audiences may already have preexisting biases for or against arguments you may make. Determining where that presumption lies and capturing the momentum of your audience's preferences to propel your arguments forward can contribute greatly to your overall strategy.[45]

Paradox #4: You're More Likely to Win by Arguing from a Difficult Position

This paradox speaks most directly to the Prime Minister's decision regarding the interpretation of the motion and that team's commitment to a position to defend. The "better debate" standard[46] of adjudication generally suggests that teams will be evaluated in part on what they do to make the debate "better." While "better" may be a vague concept, most adjudicators will acknowledge that they know a good debate when they see it: those debates tend to be the ones in which the teams engage each other directly rather than circuitously, in which the focus of the debate is on substantive issues rather than wrangling over technical matters, and in which the question posed by the motion presented is thoroughly interrogated. By contrast, the worst debates are frequently those in which one or more teams seek to gain a strategic advantage over the others by defending the narrowest ground possible in an effort to circumvent attacks from their opponents or to exclude their opponents from the debate.

Take the example case explained in Chapter 5. In a debate about the motion "This house would ban capital punishment," an Opening Proposition team may opt to define their case as a ban on the application of capital punishment to minors. The treatment of minors, they may argue, is the focus of the actual, "real-world" controversy in some areas of the United States; this interpretation addresses the critical elements of the debate about the principle behind the use of capital punishment and, as such, functions as a legitimate test of the question underlying the motion. Of course, a major (unstated) advantage of this interpretation is that such a case is significantly easier for the Proposition to prove because it so narrowly limits the ground for the debate. Rather than arguing for the merits of capital punishment in general, the Opposition — providing they choose not to object to the PM's definition — seemingly must advocate for capital punishment of minors. This more limited debate would not encompass the full range of issues implied by the original motion and would likely, therefore, be evaluated less favorably by those adjudicators who subscribe to the "better debate" standard.

But the same principle applies to the Opposition in this situation. Under WUDC rules, the Leader of the Opposition could object to the PM's interpretation.[47] The principle expressed in this paradox, however, would indicate that such an objection would be a mistake. The Leader of the Opposition—and by extension, the entire Opposition bench—would likely benefit from the adjudicators' preference for substantive debate over technical debate, and from the adjudicators' admiration for the nerve of a team that would willingly take on an argumentative burden as significant as arguing *for* putting minors to death. In other words, by adopting what likely is the more difficult route, the Opposition's success is more probable.

Finally, you can apply this principle to nearly any situation wherein you are presented with the choice between what appears to be the more defensible ground and what appears to be a more difficult position to prove. In most cases, regardless of your position in the debate, you will be more able to prove your competence as a debater by taking the tougher position and nearly making the mark than choosing the easier stance and easily proving its truth.

Paradox #5: Your Advocacy Is More Likely to Prevail if You Appear Disinterested in Winning

There's something to be said for the credibility of those who appear nonpartisan in a heated conflict. These people, be they impartial third parties, objective expert witnesses, or neutral bystanders, are those to whom we turn when we want the actual truth in a situation sorely lacking "unspun" positions. In much the same way, adjudicators are aware of the effect of partisanship on the arguments debaters make: they know that debaters will often say what they must to win a round. They realize that debaters are trained to make even questionable positions sound compelling. And as such, they are necessarily (and correctly) suspicious of the quality of any debater's arguments.

Successful debaters may overcome this inherent suspicion by presenting arguments that appear more objective than positional. Whether by adjusting the content and focus of an appeal or by carefully monitoring the presentation of that appeal, such an approach can have significant impact on your credibility.

In Chapter 3, I discuss how this principle can be applied by using "Nature of . . ." positions. By presenting the foundation of a controversial argument in a point separated from that argument, these positions can give the appearance of objectivity to the analysis and, therefore, make the argument more credible. Moreover, by acknowledging that a particular piece of evidence may be interpreted in ways both favorable to and contrary to your position, you may deflect some of the adjudicators' natural suspicion of that argument, not to mention undercutting your opponents by being the first to point out a possible alternate interpretation. In short, rather than attempting to hide from anticipated opposition attacks, and thereby appearing scared of, ignorant of, or unwilling to face such attacks, you can gain in a debate by acknowledging the other side of the issue.

This principle also applies to your conduct and demeanor in a round. Far from the raging demagogue persona most people associate with successful debaters, winning debaters frequently benefit from adoption of a more cool, detached style. This is not to say that they benefit from being disinterested; quite the contrary. You should recognize, however, that sometimes the most passionate delivery of an argument is motivated by an underlying lack of confidence in its power. If you are certain of your position (and want your audience to be as certain of your position), you may benefit more from a calm, rational, and objective tone in your presentation. This is particularly the case when you face an opponent's trembling invective. In such cases, trying to "out-passion" the other side is often a mistake. Meeting a frothing, flailing opponent with a coolly dispassionate style can often disarm him and relieve overwhelmed adjudicators.

This is one of the most challenging paradoxes for debaters to accept. Though you're required to vigorously defend your position, you'll often benefit from approaching that charge from the position of analyst rather than advocate.

Paradox #6: The More We Strive to Reduce Uncertainty through Debate, the More Uncertain We Become

The final paradox doesn't offer a great deal of insight into how to win a debate round *per se*. At least, it doesn't offer a direct recommendation about how you can position yourself to win the round. Instead, this paradox offers a way to evaluate the benefits of debating that some may find more rewarding than the transient satisfaction borne of winning a round or a tournament.

Bertrand Russell is credited with once saying that the trouble with the world is that the ignorant are cocksure and the intelligent are full of doubt. Nowhere is this more true than in the activity of debating.

There seems to be a curvilinear relationship between the amount of time spent debating and the strength of one's convictions: the more time you spend debating the more aware you become of the validity of different positions, particularly those contrary to your own.

Though debate is an exercise designed to reduce uncertainty, at its best it increases it. When we engage in debate, we typically do so with the belief that the best ideas will prevail. Underlying this assumption is the recognition that we really don't know—at least going into a debate round—which side is "right." We trust in the adversarial process to position arguments against their converse, testing the strength of any position against its diametric opposite. In so doing, debate should produce more certainty about the prevailing ideas: those that survive the test should, ostensibly, be the best.

But in the best of debates—whether they happen in debating tournaments, legislative bodies, or between friends over a pint of beer—the outcome is decidedly less certain. In the face of criticism of our arguments, we should become more flexible and open to the possibility that what we believe is fallible and, perhaps more importantly, to the possibility that what our opponents believe is not wrong.

This paradox, then, represents perhaps the noblest goal of debating: to erase the rigidity that underpins fundamentalism of any sort. When viewed through this lens, debating becomes much more than merely amassing a winning record or a full trophy cabinet: it is an exercise in opening our minds and perspectives to competing truths. When we do this, we engage in winning debates.

CHAPTER 8

Advanced Tactics

One of the most compelling aspects of debate is the creativity it inspires in its participants. Behind the innovation brought to debates by those who participate is the competitive motive: debates offer near-immediate feedback on argumentative techniques. Debaters know very quickly — usually immediately following the round — if their efforts were successful. This tight feedback loop, combined with the frequency of opportunity to practice new argumentative approaches in the laboratory that is competitive debating, produces innovative and effective strategies.

In this chapter I will discuss six advanced tactics that have proved themselves over time to be powerful approaches to presenting arguments. I've divided them into two categories: offensive tactics and defensive tactics. While these tactics don't work every time and are not useful in every situation, they are effective and universal enough to warrant their inclusion here.

My intent in presenting these tactics is not to encourage their use *per se*. Of course, if you find the approaches intuitive and the outcomes beneficial, feel free to do so. Ultimately, though, I hope to inspire others to contribute to the conversation about what works in argumentation and what doesn't. I look forward not to seeing these tactics in competition (I see them enough with my own team) but to seeing what others do using these tactics as a starting point for their own innovation.

Offensive Tactics

The time-worn belief that the best defense is a good offense is widely accepted in competitive debating. The effort at constructive argumentation—to identify, develop, and advance arguments—is typically the defining effort of a team. Indeed, the strategy of control I advocated in Chapter 4 depends on being in command of the arguments in the debate and compelling your opponents and adjudicators to focus on those arguments.

The first three tactics are directly related to constructing compelling arguments. None of these strategies exist in a vacuum; all are part of a larger, coordinated campaign of arguments to prove a point. By themselves, these tactics probably won't win debates. The tactics may, however, be a critical part of your overall constructive effort.

CAPTURING PRESUMPTION

The concept of presumption has long been recognized as a critical part of argument theory. Since Richard Whatley discussed the concept—and its attendant idea, the burden of proof—in the 19th century,[48] argument scholars have recognized the critical importance of understanding where the audience's sympathies lie.

Presumption refers to the prevailing sentiments of an audience with regard to an argument they're asked to accept. To say an argument has presumption with an audience is to say that the audience—though open to contrary positions—is predisposed to agree with that argument. An advocate who argues in favor of increasing pay for teachers before a teachers' union enjoys significant presumption for her arguments. Those who advocate positions *against* an audience's presumption bear the *burden of proof*; those with the burden of proof have a more difficult time demonstrating that their claim(s) should be accepted. In the context of a debate, the side that bears the burden of proof faces increased scrutiny in the eyes of the adjudicators, while the side with presumption enjoys the benefit of the adjudicators' inclination toward their argument.

Presumption may be either organic or synthetic. Organic presumption grows from the values, beliefs, and perspectives of an audience. If an audience, for example, comes from a liberal democratic society and believes freedom of expression to be a vital element of democratic governance, an argument that claims to protect free expression is likely to be received favorably by that audience. Those arguing for a restriction on free expression would bear a relatively higher burden of proof in such an exchange.

Some venues of argument, on the other hand, rely on synthetic presumption, or presumption created for arguments from a certain side. Criminal justice systems frequently operate on the presumption that the accused is presumed innocent until proven guilty (by the state, which bears the burden of proof). While it may be painfully obvious to some in a criminal trial that the accused is guilty, presumption of innocence is accorded to the defense to preserve the rights of the accused.

Neither organic nor synthetic presumption is fixed. Though presumption — particularly organic presumption — is grounded in the general preferences of an audience, it is malleable and subject to persuasive efforts. As such, you can capture presumption to capture the adjudicators' preference for your arguments.

Capturing presumption begins with placing the particular decision the adjudicators are asked to make in a larger context. That context could consider the general type of decision being made; previous, similar decisions that have been made; and the values that guide decision making in this instance. Typically, arguments about the location of presumption are presented early in the case and, if made convincingly, orient the adjudicators favorably toward the arguments that follow. An effective argument that enjoys presumption may be grounded in various starting points:

1. **Frameworks**. Often, the decision posed by a motion in a debate round is identifiable as a particular type of decision: in general, the debate may concern a public policy decision (many motions do) but more specifically, the debate may focus on a particular type of public policy decision. Medical questions, security issues, educational policies, legal arguments, and economic matters, for example, all have general frameworks in which such decisions are made. These frameworks serve as a guide for the values likely at issue in the decision and a preferred course of action (or at least a preferred set of guiding principles) in operation for the decision-making process.

   Consider a debate about whether to permit medical research involving human subjects in developing nations. A clear, well-established framework like the Helsinki Declaration would serve as a solid foundation for establishing presumption in a debate about this motion.[49] This document, produced to establish ethical standards for those who engage in research on human subjects, serves as a broadly accepted set of guiding principles for decisions regarding research on human subjects. The declaration makes clear that while research is important, the researcher's first priority is to the subject or volunteer, and that the subject's welfare supersedes the benefit of the research to the larger society. In a debate, the Helsinki Declaration could be referenced as a touchstone for determining the desirability of the motion.

2. **Precedence**. Analogical reasoning — to find similarities between two things in an effort to understand one or both of those things better — is a fundamental logical approach. As a basis for presumption, analogies serve as points of reference from which we can explore unknown circumstances: if a similar decision has been made successfully in the past, the presumption is that the present decision should be made in a similar way. The role of analogies in setting presumption cannot be overstated. Indeed, in legal systems based on common law — particularly the legal system of the United States — the principle of *stare decisis* establishes the strong presumption that precedents should be respected. If a matter has been settled in a previous decision, says this legal principle, that decision should stand. This same approach may be brought to bear in an argument designed for a public audience: an advocate for the importance of protecting the right of free speech — even something as objectionable as hate speech — would likely reference the reasoning of the U.S. Supreme Court's famous decision in which it affirmed the right of the Nazi party to stage a political rally in Skokie, Illinois. This precedent, the advocate would argue, clearly places a strong preference for allowing speech to occur on the side of those arguing for free speech protections.

    Of course, whether the present decision is similar (or similar enough) to previous decisions is subject to argument. To employ analogies successfully to capture presumption, you must choose an analogical precedent carefully; obviously, the precedent should have been resolved in the way you want the present decision to be rendered, but beyond that, you should look for the greatest similarity possible when selecting the analogy. When arguing the precedent, you must take care to define clearly the relationship between the present decision and the precedent, highlighting the similarities and explaining the differences. Merely saying, "This is just like the case of . . ." is rarely sufficient to establish presumption for your position. In the Skokie example, the advocate would gain more traction with her audience if she explained that the Nazi party, much like those whose hate speech is threatened with sanction, sought to generalize (unfavorably, obviously) about specific ethnic minorities as a central tenet of their message. The advocate would likely contend that such speech — which the U.S. Supreme Court found worthy of protecting — is no different than the "hate speech" that various groups want to ban.

3. **Values**. As noted above, organic presumption is grounded in the beliefs and orientations of the audience. In some cases, you may capture considerable presumption for your position by affiliating that position with a particular value orientation you know your audience embraces.[50] Alternately, you may identify a presumptive value orientation that you can argue *is or should be* relevant to a particular decision. In either case, connecting the immediate decision to an enduring principle or broadly accepted moral imperative can incline the adjudicators' preference toward your argument.

Consider a debate over the motion "This house would ignore national boundaries to implement humanitarian objectives." A debater can make the case against this position stronger by arguing that the value of national sovereignty must be paramount. If the adjudicators are inclined to value the preservation of national sovereignty above all else, they are likely to look favorably on this argument.

ESTABLISHING URGENCY

The very nature of the decisions made in BP debating demands that advocates establish the urgency of their proposals. Most BP debates concern decisions about whether or not to take some action. The policy motions for these debates typically are phrased as propositions about what we should do: "This house would legalize all recreational drugs" or "This house would refuse to broadcast videos produced by terrorists" are good examples of the types of issues considered in BP debates.

Usually these propositions are phrased as departures from the status quo. In contrast to the way things are done now, such motions ask, "Is there a better way?" Creating change, convincing others to do something differently, faces not only the obstacle of the unknown but the inertia of the past. To make a case for change in public policy requires not only a good reason to do so but proof that a unique occasion exists for us to make such a change.

Rhetorical theorists have long recognized the power of establishing the immediacy of an appeal. Ancient Greek rhetoricians discussed the importance of *kairos*, the "exceptionality of opportunity," in which an oratorical effort must be positioned. The principle of *kairos* dictated that a speech should be grounded in some critical moment, some occasion that makes this the appropriate and inevitable time for the appeal. Modern rhetorical scholars such as Lloyd Bitzer also discussed the role that occasion plays in compelling messages when he included exigence as an essential element of what he called the "rhetorical situation."[51] In such situations, an exigence serves as the motive for the persuasive plea. Exigence both presents the opportunity for the change sought and positions the appeal at the critical moment for that change. Clearly, establishing your position as the "right option at the right time" has long been recognized as a technique to empower your persuasive appeal.

Creating urgency for your position is powerful because it allows you to present your appeal as one positioned at a critical juncture, uniquely poised for success and distinct from the conventional criticisms traditionally levied at options usually considered in such controversies. Consider the motion "This house would require the producers of meat products to include realistic depictions of the slaughter process on their products' packaging." This motion asks that the Proposition defend a policy that seeks to minimize cruelty to animals but refrains from calling for the outright prohibition of slaughter. Developing a strong sense of *kairos* can make the appeal more compelling.

To do so, you would develop an entire point early in your case that places this decision in its exigent context: you may argue that we have come far in our appreciation for animal rights, with legislation to prevent deliberate and outright cruelty to animals, a greater appreciation for animals as creatures with sentient characteristics, and broad consumer demand for more humane treatment of animals in the food production industry (such as the "free range" designation given to certain animal products). With that established, you would then contend that in spite of the progress we have made, we have not yet reached consensus as a society that the consumption of meat is intolerable. Indeed, the majority of people still consider meat an irreplaceable part of their daily diet. While we may be on a trajectory toward one day recognizing that consuming meat is immoral, we have not yet arrived at that conclusion.

Thus, you would claim, the stage has been set for a change like the one represented in the proposition. To publicize the slaughter process is an advance in policy that is consistent with the trend in this area (and therefore is empowered by the presumptive momentum of moral evolution) and that takes a step of appropriate scale, without attempting to accomplish more than current public sentiment would find suitable for the present circumstance.

The power of this approach lies, in large part, in its ability to create space in which your opponents' arguments may exist, albeit in a diminished state. Rather than contending that your opponents' arguments are untrue, you may say that they are simply no longer timely and relevant to your position. In the above example, Opposition arguments seeking to demonstrate that animals shouldn't be accorded rights may be diminished by referring to the trend toward a greater appreciation for animal rights. You needn't prove that animals *have* rights (i.e., you needn't prove that your opponents' argument is false), merely that the argument that animals *don't* have rights is no longer generally accepted. The same approach mitigates opposing arguments that claim that dire consequences will result from extending rights to animals or that claim that providing for more humane treatment is economically crippling to producers. These arguments may once have held weight, you may contend, but given the background and trajectory of the controversy—that we have recognized some animal rights without catastrophic consequences—they are no longer of great concern. By allowing for the possibility that what your opponents argue may have been true *in the past*, you avoid the burden of proving that your opposition is wrong (and therefore appear to be more tolerant, inclusive, informed, and, ultimately, credible).

Developing urgency, then, depends on defining the past and present in an effort to identify the present moment as the inevitable instant of change. Often, establishing a trajectory of events may demonstrate the aptness of the change; to show that the change has been coming for a time inclines the audience toward that change. Similarly, a crisis may present an opportune moment during which significant change may be enacted. In any case, placing your advocacy in context, demonstrating the uniqueness of the moment, and motivating your audience to act based on the novelty of occasion can add power and dynamism to your case.

EMPLOYING OBJECTIVITY

One of the obstacles debaters face is their adjudicators' suspicion of their motives and, therefore, their arguments. Adjudicators, trained to be hypercritical consumers of argument, are naturally skeptical of any argument advanced by a debater because of the inherently partisan nature of the exercise. Adjudicators assume that debaters want to win rounds and will therefore represent (if not misrepresent) information in a way most conducive to that goal.

Successful debaters overcome this innate suspicion by employing tactics that downplay the inherent subjectivity of their arguments. One of these tactics—known colloquially as a "Nature of . . ." position— works by presenting important foundational arguments in a way that appears objective and disinterested. By presenting the information as "just the facts" and divorcing the foundational argument from the explicit appeal for (or against) the motion, the "Nature of . . ." position both allows for the full development of a concept without attracting significant scrutiny and camouflages the importance of that concept to your overall strategy. "Nature of . . ." arguments typically come in one of three forms:

1. **Principle**. These arguments establish some well-accepted principle that serves as a guiding point for evaluation. That principle could emerge from some well-accepted moral imperative (like "defending liberty" or "respecting sovereignty") or it could emerge from analogous cases or precedents in which a decision has been rendered in favor of the type of position you advocate. A case arguing that we should not employ racial profiling in the so-called Global War on Terror may begin with a point entitled "The nature of equal protection under the law." That principle, once explained and substantiated, would serve as a foundation for a rejection of a discriminatory police practice. Later arguments in the case would seek to demonstrate the various ways racial profiling violates the equal protection principle.

   The effectiveness of the tactic lies in investing heavily in what appears to be a simple presentation of noncontroversial background information: in the racial profiling example, the first point is merely an objective recitation of a legal principle relevant to the decision under consideration. Once you have established that equal protection is an important and relevant concept (which, objectively speaking, it is), the heavy lifting of the case has already been done. The next step, affiliating racial profiling with that principle, is a relatively easy task.

2. **Causal**. Causal arguments unpack the underlying relational con-
    nections between critical elements of the debate. Establishing the
    causal connections between phenomena is a difficult task in any
    context. In a debate — with opponents on the ready to refute your
    every argument — it is an extraordinary challenge. Presenting the
    causal analysis required of a particular case as a "Nature of . . ." po-
    sition can help to insulate your arguments from intense scrutiny.

    Consider a motion such as "This house would ban violent me-
    dia." Any case arguing for such restrictions will have to prove
    that violence in media causes real-world violence. Rather than
    attempting to link the consumption of violent media to violent
    behavior directly, you could open your case with a point enti-
    tled "The nature of media influence." In that point, you would
    outline the causal connections between behavior observed in
    the media and the corresponding actual behaviors: the success
    of advertising, for example, proves that the media is capable
    of influencing behavior. This evidence, and other support that
    speaks to the influence of media in general, serves as a more
    objective — and therefore more credible — treatment of the re-
    lationship between media and behavior. As with the previous
    example, later points in the case would be developed to address
    the impacts of violence in the media, but the groundwork for
    the causal point — likely the most vulnerable point in the case —
    has already been laid.

3. **Analytic**. Analytic "Nature of . . ." positions outline the features
    and attributes of a critical element of the debate in an effort to
    cast that element in a certain light. As discussed in Chapter 2,

debates may revolve around not only the relationship between things and the value of things but also the very description of the things about which we're debating.

In general, analytic "Nature of . . ." positions recognize that the description of the thing about which we're debating is intimately linked with our evaluation of that thing. Remember that most debates ultimately focus on the evaluation of some thing, be it a policy or a course of action. Describing what that thing is — particularly in a way that appears disconnected from the attempt to prove that the thing is good or bad — can be a powerful tactic for predisposing your audience toward your evaluative effort.

By way of example, imagine you've been assigned to prove that the UN should not intervene in the Darfur region of Sudan. Your case against UN intervention in Sudan might begin with an analysis of "the nature of the UN military intervention." This point could establish the extraordinary obstacles faced by the UN Security Council in authorizing military intervention, the typical lack of political will evinced by members of the UN to intervene militarily, and the historical failures of UN intervention. By presenting the position as a broad and historical description of UN intervention, the ultimate goal of the arguments — to prove that UN intervention in Sudan is undesirable — is obscured. When you proceed in the following points of your case to establish how intervention in Sudan would be subject to the same obstacles, politics, and likely failure as other efforts, proving the UN should not do so is much easier.

Offensive tactics allow you to present your constructive arguments in a way most likely to serve your strategy of control in the round. By themselves, however, offensive tactics are incomplete. In addition to advancing your own arguments in a debate, you must manage the arguments made by others in that round.

Defensive Tactics

To call the next three tactics "defensive" is to risk giving the wrong impression of their utility. By labeling them defensive, I do not mean to imply that they are second-line choices, to be used when the offensive tactics are not available. Nor do I intend to suggest that these are tactics you may scramble toward in an emergency, when you are placed "on the defensive" by your opponents.

Instead, to call these tactics defensive is to indicate that they are most useful in managing your interactions with your opponents' arguments. In good rounds, against good teams, you must deal with the offensive efforts of your opponents. These three tactics provide options for managing your strategy in relation to your opponents' offense.

BALANCING INTERESTS

Governments exist—in part—to manage the conflicts that erupt among the governed. When your vision of what our collective future should be is different from mine, we find in the process of governance the means by which to reconcile our competing views of what's right, desirable, and necessary. In such governments, the legislative process (at least as it is designed to work in functioning liberal democratic governments) employs the tools of persuasion, compromise, and collaboration to reach a decision that seeks to satisfy the competing desires of the various parties involved. Effective policy making is predicated on the assumption that this process leads the parties to a natural state of balance between their competing claims.

Good policy making requires accommodation of competing parties and their interests: if one constituency advocates for increased government access to private citizens' information so that law enforcement agencies can better identify and apprehend those that intend harm to the country, another constituency will likely argue that such a proposal would violate the privacy of the very citizens the government seeks to protect. Both parties have a legitimate concern. In this case, the proposal arrived at through the legislative process likely would be one that balances the concerns of both sides by providing for the most security while preserving the maximum privacy. That solution is the product of persuasion (convincing the other side of the virtue of your position), compromise (trading concessions for gains), and collaboration (a willingness to work with the other party to achieve your goals).

Perhaps unfortunately, debate is not an activity that encourages cooperation and compromise in the pursuit of the best policy. In a debate, the adjudicators play the role of the policy-making authority (they decide which position will prevail) while the competing sides represent the parties and positions with a concern in the outcome of the debate. For most debaters, vigorous representation of those positions translates into a polarized, positional effort to defend your perspective while undermining your opponents' positions. Adjudicators are not permitted to vote for part of one side's proposal and part of the other side's, even though such an approach would likely create the best public policy.

This contradiction between real-world policy making and debating about policies puts adjudicators in a difficult position. Many rounds leave adjudicators convinced that both sides make compelling arguments. In a roundabout development of fossil-fuel resources, for example, an adjudicator may be convinced that new development of fossil fuel resources is both necessary to meet energy demands and likely to produce significant economic benefits for the state that owns those re-sources. Simultaneously, the same adjudicator may be convinced that development of those resources will have an irreversible impact on the environment, both through the process of extracting the oil, coal, or natural gas and through the carbon released when they're burned. If both positions are true, for which side should the adjudicators decide?

Winning debaters can make use of the tactics and tools of real-world policy making while tapping into the natural inclination of ad-judicators to give credence to both sides' arguments. To prevail in a debate where the adjudicators may be inclined to see the legitimacy of both sides' positions, you need to convince the adjudicators that your position best accommodates the various (legitimate) interests of all parties involved in the controversy. To do so, you develop a position in three steps:

1. **Identify stakeholders and their interests**. The stakeholders are those who will be affected by the policy decision under consid-eration. The stakeholders typically are groups, organizations, or institutions united by their interests. Interests, simply put, are what the stakeholders desire: adherence to principles, preserva-tion of values, and specific, tangible outcomes usually define a stakeholder's interests. To convince the adjudicators that your po-sition best balances the competing interests of those stakeholders involved in the controversy, you must first make explicit who they are and what they want.

   Consider a debate on the motion "This house would prohibit the advertisement of alcoholic beverages." In this controversy the stakeholders are loosely gathered into two groups: those who would propose that alcohol ads be banned and those who would oppose such a ban. Both stakeholders have interests that motivate their participation in the conflict: the "pro-ban" group—likely made up of parents, consumer advocates, physicians, social workers, and others—want to minimize the harmful impact of alcohol on individuals and society. Those opposed to the ban—such as alcohol producers, distributors, and retailers—want to preserve their right to sell their legal product.

In the first step of using the balancing argument, you must identify and discuss the stakeholders and their interest so adjudicators can appreciate the legitimacy of their interests and therefore the desirability of endorsing the position that best balances their desires. Identifying stakeholders and their interests in the controversy sets the stage for you to convince the adjudicators that the position you support best meets the desires of both.

2. **Describe how the opposing side's advocacy results in imbalance**. After you have outlined the interests of each stakeholder, your next step is to explain how your opponents' position results in a state of imbalance between the stakeholders. Clearly identifying your opponents' position and demonstrating how it would tip the balance in favor of one stakeholder while ignoring the interests of others demonstrates to the adjudicators that your opponents are not giving due consideration to all legitimate claims in the controversy.

    Let's assume that you're assigned to propose the "ban alcohol ads" motion. The default position of the Opposition is the status quo: currently, the advertisement of alcohol products is legal;

those who oppose a ban on the advertisement of alcohol products would prefer that advertising remain legal. The Opposition's position, you would argue, privileges the interests of those opposed to regulating the sale of alcohol over those with a legitimate interest in mitigating the impacts that alcohol use (and abuse) has on society. In other words, in the status quo, those who profit from the sale of alcohol get everything they want (to market and sell their product), but those concerned about the impact of alcohol get little of what they want (to curb alcohol's impact).

Demonstrating that your opponent's position does not consider the interests of a legitimate party to the controversy is relatively easy. The balancing tactic requires, though, that in doing so you're careful not to intimate that the other stakeholder's interests (i.e., those represented by your opponents) are not legitimate. Remember that the strategy depends on balancing the competing interests in the conflict; recognizing the legitimacy of those interests is a prerequisite to balancing them. Your approach will not be to prove that alcohol is evil and a bane to all those who use it, but that the status quo — which allows the alcohol industry to create sometimes excessive or inappropriate demand for its product — doesn't recognize the valid claims of those who want to reduce the impact of alcohol. Acknowledging the legitimacy of interests of all parties involved and demonstrating how your opponents' position creates an imbalance between those interests sets the stage for the final step in the process.

3. **Explain how your side produces better balance among stakeholders**. With an eye toward recognizing the legitimacy of each

side, it's now time to explain to the adjudicators why your position better balances both stakeholders' interests.

In our example (in which you're arguing for a ban on alcohol ads), you would argue that a ban on advertisement of alcohol products meets the interests of those dedicated to minimizing alcohol's impact on society while allowing the alcohol industry to continue to profit from the sale of its product. In so doing, the position represents a functional compromise between the interests of the two competing parties: the "pro-ban" group would likely prefer that all alcohol be banned; the "anti-ban" group would prefer that the sale and advertisement of alcohol products remain legal. This compromise, while not fulfilling the entirety of either stakeholder's interests, is desirable because it reconciles those interests in a way that recognizes the legitimacy of both.

While this example imagines the tactic being employed by a Proposition team, it is equally powerful (perhaps even more so) for an Opposition team. On Opposition, the position you'll typically advocate will be either the status quo or a counterproposal — some policy change that is different from and exclusive to the proposal offered by the other team. In any case, your proposal should be a course of action that more evenly balances the interests of all stakeholders.

The power of this strategy is that it creates room for your opponents' arguments while still giving the adjudicators reason to prefer your advocacy. Given that most rounds will feature compelling arguments presented by skilled debaters, it is unlikely that adjudicators will be excited about an outright rejection of those arguments. This option allows a team to recognize the authority of their opponents' arguments (or at least their interests) while presenting an alternative that better preserves the various legitimate priorities of all parties involved.

GOALS ANALYSIS

At its core, debating is decision making. Of the elements of the decision-making process discussed in Chapter 6, perhaps the most significant was the goal; the goals we seek define the decisions we make. Of course, as you have seen, the goals in operation in any act of decision making are rarely clear. We tend to operate on a variety of motives, some more explicit than others. This is no different in competitive debating. Most teams build their advocacy for a position around a list of "good reasons" to prefer the stance they represent. This approach is often successful simply because, with many different arguments for a position, the adjudicators are likely to find something they like.

A powerful tactic for dealing with your opponents' constructive arguments is also a quite simple one: it begins with making explicit what your opponents seek to achieve. Once this goal (or these goals) has been identified, you are better equipped to manage your opponents' arguments and your own strategy.

Discerning Goals

Goals come in two forms: primary goals and ancillary goals. Primary goals are the chief reason to enact a proposal; typically, primary goals relate to the resolution of some problem. Primary goals tend to be easy to identify, whether or not the team has made the goal explicit in their case. In many cases, however, teams may offer a series of goals they seek to accomplish; these goals are typically above and beyond addressing the most obvious problem that would be resolved by enacting the policy. When making a case for opening more federal lands to oil exploration, for example, advocates typically rely on arguments such as meeting current energy needs, decreasing dependency on foreign sources of oil, economic development from jobs and oil revenue, and other such reasons. In this case, each of these reasons serves as a goal that is arguably ancillary to the primary goal of discovering more energy resources. The goal analysis tactic is most effective when you can articulate a primary goal and treat other goals as ancillary.

Identifying your opponents' primary goal(s) may be as simple as listening to them. Some teams articulate a stated objective (what they hope to accomplish with their proposal) as part of their prospective framing. If, for example, a team proposing a ban on cigarette sales opened their arguments by saying, "We offer this plan with the aim of curbing smoking—both for current and potential smokers," the primary goal they're seeking is obvious.

In other cases, however, the primary goal is less clear, either because the team has failed to make it so or they have multiple goals. If this is the case, you must identify and express their primary goal. This is not to imply that you misrepresent their goal; quite the opposite. Identifying a primary goal either from a variety of goals or from an unclear case requires that you seek an appropriate level of abstraction of their goal that will encompass the various goals they have articulated. Using the above example, you might approach a case about opening federal lands to oil exploration by identifying as the primary goal "increasing energy resources," an expression of a primary goal that encapsulates the ancillary goals of meeting energy needs, decreasing dependence on foreign sources, and the economic growth that comes from development of resources.

Countering Arguments with Goal Analysis

Once you have identified the primary goal, you can use that goal to demonstrate that your opponents' proposal is undesirable. Typically, you can use five approaches—employed alone or in concert with one another—to prove this point:

1. Mitigation. Mitigation seeks to demonstrate that the proposal won't accomplish the goal or won't accomplish the goal in a significant way. Mitigation tactics seek to disrupt the causal claims of the effect the proposal will have. In most cases, mitigation at best demonstrates that the proposal won't have as dramatic an effect as its proponents claim. Take, for example, a case advocating making the production, sale, and consumption of tobacco illegal. The Proposition's primary goal is curbing smoking. To mitigate the Proposition's claim that their policy will diminish smoking, those opposing would point out that tobacco is engrained in our culture, much more so than even other banned substances. You might argue that in the case of the other banned substances, those determined to consume them have always found willing suppliers of the substances: witness the failure of the so-called war on drugs in the United States. At best, you would claim, the proposal would result in a minimal decline in the numbers of people consuming tobacco.

By itself, mitigation is rarely a successful strategy. As noted above, typically the best common outcome of mitigation is that significance of the effect is diminished. For example, after your mitigation efforts, the Proposition might adjust its position and argue that *some* smokers will be deterred. Obviously, with some solvency still intact the adjudicators still have reason to favor the proposal. Mitigation is most effective when presented in concert with one of the remaining approaches.

2. Contravention. Arguing that a proposal may not be as effective as your opponents claim (mitigation) is not as powerful as arguing that your opponents' proposal will actually move them farther from their goal. As an approach, contravention seeks to demonstrate that not only do things not get better but they actually get worse with the Proposition's proposal.

In the above oil exploration example, the proposal to open federal lands to oil development sought to meet the goal of expanding energy resources. If they opt to argue that such a policy actually contravenes the goal sought, the Opposition team may claim that new development of oil resources only delays research and development of alternative renewable energy sources, thereby actually decreasing our total available energy resources. While it may appear in the short term that we have more energy by drilling new wells, claims the Opposition, in reality we'll only delay the crisis that may actually produce new forms of energy, thus contravening the Proposition's goal.

3. Consequences. All proposals have effects. Proponents of such proposals claim that those effects meet the goals they pursue. Opponents may gain ground by arguing that regardless of whether the primary goal sought by their opponents is met, the consequences of enacting the proposed policy render that policy undesirable.

Consequences are arguments you build around the dismal things that happen when the proposal is adopted. In the oil development example, an Opposition team could offer an extended analysis of the environmental impacts of extracting oil from wilderness areas, as well as the environmental impacts of burning more fossil fuels. If rendered compellingly, such calamitous consequences could create significant reservations in the adjudicators' minds.

4. Alternative proposal. Once you have demonstrated the undesirability of your opponents' proposal, a powerful option is to offer an alternative proposal that will better meet their goal. To propose an alternative, you must first establish that your opponents' proposal is undesirable either because it will not achieve the goal or because of the consequences of enacting the proposal. In either (or both) cases, you are creating the desire for an alternative in the minds of your adjudicators.

Alternative proposals are most effective when they create an either-or choice for the adjudicators: in other words the adjudicators cannot opt for *both* proposals. Choosing an alternative proposal that is mutually exclusive with your opponents' proposal creates such a choice. The importance of this element may be demonstrated with the consideration of an alternative proposal that is not exclusive with an opponents' proposal. If, in the oil development example, you proposed that instead of drilling for more oil we should subsidize the development of alternative energies, you would not have created an either-or choice for your adjudicators. In other words, what's to prevent the proponents of drilling from encouraging the adjudicators to favor both? If your opponents argue that we ought to develop fossil fuel resources as a stopgap measure while developing alternatives, your adjudicators may be convinced that we can do both and, therefore, vote for the drilling proposal (since the question before the house is specific to development of oil resources). Clearly, an alternative that is mutually exclusive to your opponents' proposal is most effective.

5. Alternative goal. Finally, you have the option of arguing that your opponents' goal is inappropriate (or at least should not be the primary goal). In my opinion, this approach is the least effective use of goal analysis. Nothing is more compelling than conceding the worth of your opponents' goal and then demonstrating that they don't achieve it.

If, however, you are unable to connect your deconstruction of their position to the goal they seek, your best option may be to advocate for an alternate goal. Note that this approach is virtually identical to the devices available to your when comparing your goal hierarchy to your opponents' goals hierarchy (see Chapter 6). This approach is most effective when you choose a goal that is more significant than your opponents'. In our oil development example, an alternate goal could be the protection and reparation of the environment. This goal, you may argue, outweighs concerns about the availability of energy because the environment is the foundation of our very existence. Without a healthy environment, our concerns for available energy seem trivial.

The reason the goal analysis tactic is so effective is because it so closely parallels the natural course of decision making we discussed earlier. By building a strategy that has at its center the consideration of the goal sought and the potential for the proposal to meet that goal, you make explicit the elements and process of decision making the adjudicators will naturally employ. Clear analysis of these elements allows you to have more control over that process.

Implicit Collusion

I'm asking for trouble with the name of this defensive tactic, but allow me to explain. Collusion — that is, explicit collusion between teams in a debate — is unethical and must be avoided. By explicit collusion I mean those behaviors in which two or more teams conspire to cooperate — rather than compete — to their mutual advantage. Preparing together before the round, disclosing positions to provide additional time to design responses, agreeing to misrepresent factual information, and the like are all examples of collusion that are contrary to the ethical principles of debating.

That said, the presence of four teams in a British Parliamentary debate and the reward structure of ordinal rankings for individual teams present tactical opportunities that allow you to better control the adjudicators' perception of the round.

I call this tactic *implicit* collusion because the act of "collusion" is unilateral — and therefore by definition *not* an act of collusion. The tactic achieves outcomes, however, that are functionally similar to those that might be achieved if teams did engage in explicit conspiracy with one another. As such, it is a powerful tactic that doesn't engender the ethical consequences of cheating.

In brief, implicit collusion is a strategic choice to engage the arguments of another, particular team in the round while minimizing the efforts of the remaining teams. As noted above, unlike binary debating, BP debating concludes with the adjudicators ranking the four teams in the round from best to worst; in strict competitive terms (and, indeed, in terms of the record usually needed to advance to elimination rounds), the first- and second-place rankings constitute a "win" while the third-and fourth-place rankings are a "loss." This reward structure presents an unmistakable opportunity: if you can affiliate yourself with a particular team — and thereby make your interactions with that team the primary focus of the adjudicators' attention while diminishing the contributions of the other teams in the round — you stand a significantly better chance of being ranked in the top half of the round.

Implicit collusion involves two steps: locating the strategic correlation between your team and another team in the round and then emphasizing that correlation.

1. **Locating the strategic correlation.** Identifying the team with whom you have the best chances of developing a strategic correlation is far more art than science. To direct the adjudicators' attention toward the most important arguments in a round, you must first be able to recognize them. Two types of alliance are possible: alliances with teams "on the same bench" and "cross-aisle" alliances.

    Coalitions with teams on the same bench (i.e., a team on the same side of the motion) are the default strategic correlation in BP debating. As the BP format models the legislative function of coalition governments found in democracies with systems of proportional representation, teams in the opening and the closing position are expected to pursue the same general strategic orientation; namely, to support the side of the motion to which they have been assigned. That said, there is a difference between avoiding strategic choices that contradict your bench mates and making strategic choices to elevate you own strategy to the top of the round. Primarily, this difference is determined by the closing teams: if a closing team comes to believe that their best chances for success are to throw in with their opening team, they should do all they can to emphasize the significance of that team's arguments. Praising the arguments, integrating the opening team's positions into their own strategy, featuring prominently the opening team's arguments in summaries, and framing and other such strategies indicate clearly to adjudicators that the focus of their attention should be on the strategic correlation between both Proposition or both Opposition teams.

But strategic correlations may also be established with teams from across the aisle. A Closing Proposition team may opt to focus on the arguments of the Opening Opposition team rather than emphasizing the cooperation between the Proposition teams. Similarly, a Closing Opposition team may believe that the most substantial Proposition arguments come from the Opening Proposition and opt, therefore, to deemphasize the contributions from the Closing Proposition (the team against which they're typically poised) in favor of emphasizing the Opening Proposition's strategy. Another version of the cross-aisle correlation may be developed between the "top half" or "bottom half" teams. In an effort to emphasize the first four speeches or the last four speeches in the debate, implicit collusion may develop between the Closing Proposition and Closing Opposition teams or between the Opening Proposition and Opening Opposition teams.[52]

2. **Implementing the correlation**. Recognizing the potential for a strategic correlationship with another team does not guarantee that the adjudicators will appreciate the correlationship. Developing the correlationship is critical to inviting the team with whom you're seeking the correlationship to participate in the implicit collusion. Three approaches—engagement, confederacy, and "freezeout"—used alone or in concert, will help to implement the correlationship to your advantage.

Engagement refers to focusing your deconstructive efforts on a particular team's arguments. Useful only in those instances of implicit collusion with teams from across the aisle, engagement of a particular team's arguments makes those arguments more significant in the adjudicators' consideration. Ironically, focusing a deconstructive effort on a particular argument often has the effect of increasing the esteem with which the adjudicators consider that argument. By engaging a particular argument, you are implying that it is an important—and potentially threatening—position. Those arguments that go ignored are (typically) those that quickly fall out of the adjudicators' consideration.

Confederacy seeks a mutually beneficial relationship with another team. Confederacy is an obvious choice of orientation for implicit collusion with teams on your own bench. Reinforcing an opening (or closing) team's arguments that prove your side of the motion is an inherent part of the format, but you may also develop confederacy with teams across the aisle. As noted earlier, even the act of deconstructing a particular team's arguments is a form of confederacy, as it draws attention to those arguments. More subtle forms of reinforcement such as explicitly identifying a particular opponent's arguments as "critical" to the adjudicators' decision or at "the core of the issue" are examples of how you may elevate your opponent's arguments. Of course, the goal of confederacy is not to laud opposing arguments to the point that the adjudicators become convinced that they are superior to yours; even the most extreme examples of cross-aisle confederacy are enacted by teams that want to be ranked first in the round. Rather, you are looking to seek a balance where your respect for your opponent's arguments demonstrates that you—better than the other teams in the round—recognize the most critical points of stasis in the debate.

Freezeout is a controversial but necessary part of the implicit collusion strategy. Perhaps a better name for the orientation would be "constructive marginalization," wherein the contributions of some teams are downplayed while the affiliation among others is emphasized. The controversial nature of this orientation is that freezing teams out—particularly when practiced by multiple teams—takes the "frozen" team's (or those teams') performance out of their hands. Averting consideration of their contribution to the round denies them the chance to prove their worth. That said, I see such efforts to marginalize those frozen teams' contributions as no different from a (perfectly well-accepted) effort to frame the debate so that the adjudicators give their contribution less credence. Some of the ways in which teams may be frozen out of a round include directly ignoring their arguments, recasting their contributions in simplistic or humorous terms, refusing to recognize the speakers for Points of Information, placing your cursory consideration of their arguments (if you opt not to ignore them outright) in the middle of your organization, and so forth.

Finally, any effort to collude with certain teams while marginalizing others must be undertaken conservatively. Blatant opportunities to genuinely exclude other teams from the round are rare and typically arise from extreme circumstances, such as when a team has offered a position that is so exceptionally counterintuitive or offensive that it deserves little credit. Many a team has attempted to engage in implicit collusion only to lose a round to an adjudication panel that interpreted their lack of attention to certain arguments as a failure to comprehend their importance. Similarly, because the collusion is implicit, you have to constantly monitor the willingness of the target team to engage in the tactic with you. While their cooperation isn't absolutely necessary, the strategy works best when you are able to entice them to reinforce the focus of the round (between your team and the other engaged in the tactic) as the critical focus. When in doubt, engage the arguments of all teams in the round.

Ultimately, these six tactics seek to reinforce your strategy of control. Whether offensive or defensive, these tactics operate on the premise that the arguments in the round—all the arguments, yours and your opponents—are potentially under your control. With resourcefulness, innovation, and creativity, these tactics and others will help you win more debates.

CHAPTER 9

Adjudicating Debates

Who Should Read This Chapter?

Too often, chapters like this are written with the assumption that only adjudicators will read them. Perhaps this is because debaters often overlook the significance of the adjudicator in a debate. Don't get me wrong, I don't believe there exists a debater who doesn't understand that adjudicators ultimately make the decision about who lost and who won the round. This comprehension, though, doesn't seem to translate into a realization that understanding how the adjudicator makes that decision will increase significantly the chances that the decision will be in your favor.

In other words, this chapter really is perhaps more useful to debaters than to adjudicators. Careful study of how adjudicators reach their decisions will enable you to build strategies that parallel how those adjudicators think.

Finally, those looking for the advice on the practical administration of a debate round (how to call a house to order, how to announce speakers, how to take notes, etc.) will not find such advice in this chapter. With regard to Worlds-style debating, these subjects have been covered in great detail elsewhere.[53] This chapter intends to recommend a general approach to the appraisal of debates and a method for evaluating competing lines of argument made in the debate.

The Guiding Principles of Adjudication

Three principles should guide the adjudicators' appraisal of a debate:

1. An adjudicator should be ***tabula rasa*** (literally, "a blank slate") in her orientation toward the proposition;

2. An adjudicator should operate under the principle of **non-intervention** regarding the debaters' efforts; and

3. An adjudicator is first and foremost an **educator** entrusted with the responsibility of helping others improve their skills.

TABULA RASA

The metaphor of the blank slate is appropriate for the adjudicator's orientation toward the arguments made in the round. Regardless of the particular preferences for the truth or falsity of a motion, the adjudicator must—to the greatest extent possible—set aside those preferences and embrace the artifice of impartiality. Adjudicators must avoid deciding the round based on what they believed before the round occurred rather than what occurred in the round.

That said, the artifice of *tabula rasa* is just that: an artifice. Subjectivity is the defining characteristic of the human experience; not surprisingly, it simply cannot be set aside when adjudicating. A *tabula rasa* orientation is an ideal toward which an adjudicator should strive, but simultaneously that adjudicator must recognize that such impartiality will likely never be achieved.

NON-INTERVENTION

If the adjudicator is aware of the need to set aside her predispositions prior to the round, she should also be committed to avoiding intervening in the teams' efforts in the round. More to the point, non-intervention means one simple thing: adjudicators should let the debaters do the debating.

In practice, this means adjudicators must resist two temptations. First, adjudicators should avoid doing the work of the debaters. They should not complete unfinished or inadequate arguments, connect lines of argument to opposing points the debater did not recognize, or fabricate a unifying strategy for a debater's disparate arguments that was not the debater's creation. Second, and by far the more significant sin, an adjudicator must never render the debater's efforts irrelevant. Ignoring a debater's efforts is contrary to the very purpose of the activity. An adjudicator is in the round to assess the efforts of the debaters, not to selectively recognize only those efforts that she prefers. That is not to say that the adjudicator has to give equal credence to every argument made simply because a debater articulated that argument; the very purpose of adjudicating a round is to evaluate the quality of the debaters' efforts. But adjudicators should make a conscious effort to consider all arguments made to avoid inserting themselves into the round.

EDUCATION

This principle is perhaps the most important for putting the adjudicator in the appropriate frame of mind to judge a round. Debating is connected to academia for a very important reason: debating is one of the most intellectually stimulating activities an individual may undertake. Skill development in persuasive communication and critical thinking will enhance a student's academic experience across the board. For providing opportunity and motivation to enhance these skills, debating has few peers. The adjudicators should take seriously their responsibilities regarding education; decisions should honor the significant intellectual energy the debaters have expended and constructive criticism designed to help the debaters improve their skills should be paramount.

Adjudication Models

A useful way to begin thinking about your responsibilities as an adjudicator is to consider the various models of adjudication available to you. These models provide you with a general orientation and perspective from which you may assess the efforts of the debaters in the round. While none of these models is sufficient to address the complexity of rendering a decision after a debate, they do provide useful starting points for the discussion of how to do so. In general, there are two less practical and one preferred model.

LESS PRACTICAL MODELS
"Truth of Motion" Model

Adjudicators who operate under the "truth of motion" model see their role as assessing the veracity of the motion. These adjudicators see the motion as a statement with truth value (i.e., it may be either more true or more false); the defining question they ask themselves when rendering a decision is "At the end of the debate, do I believe the motion is true or false?"

This model recognizes that the debate is ultimately a contest of ideas and that the most compelling arguments should carry the day. The approach is oriented toward the *matter* of the arguments; this type of adjudicator awards the win to the team whose arguments have the most significant influence on her assessment of the truth or falsity of the motion.

The risk of this model, of course, is that the adjudicator's inherent bias may create an uneven playing field. These biases—whether explicitly acknowledged or implicit in the adjudicator's interpretation of the round—may predispose her to believe the motion is true (or false) even before a round begins. The subjective nature of the activity means that an adjudicator will likely inherently prefer one side of the motion to the other. If the adjudicator is unable to set those biases aside (and adjudicators *are* unable to do so—see the discussion of the *tabula rasa* orientation above), the result is an unfair advantage for either the Proposition or the Opposition teams.

"Skill of Debaters" Model

A contrast to the "truth of motion" model is the "skill of debaters" model. A judge who uses this model is primarily concerned with the teams' execution of their arguments and broader strategy. At the end of the round, an adjudicator using this model asks herself "Which team did the better job of debating?"

The "skill" model focuses on the *manner* of the debaters. An advantage of this focus is that a factor the debaters can control—their own performance—is the basis for the decision. Adjudicators who render decisions using this model look to criteria such as role fulfillment, speaking style, structural clarity, and engagement of the opposing teams' arguments to determine who prevailed in the round.

But the "skill of debaters" model is not without risks. Chief among the perils of this model is the possibility that a technically strong team will make inaccurate or irrelevant arguments and thus be rewarded for their presentation rather than the quality of their arguments. In other words, the best-sounding team doesn't always make the best arguments.

A Preferred Model: The "Movement" Model

The "movement" model attempts to account for the weaknesses of the two previous models by combining the best of each. It recognizes that the adjudicator's focus should be on the truth of the motion and the quality of the arguments that seek to establish that truth while also recognizing that the best efforts of the debaters — while able to make a significant impact on the adjudicator — may not result in the adjudicator changing her mind. The question the adjudicator asks herself when rendering a decision is "By the end of the round, which team moved me farthest from my original beliefs about the motion?"

Imagine the adjudicator's conviction as a point on a continuum; most adjudicators will have an opinion about the truth of the motion prior to the round. Before the round, the adjudicator's belief about the truth of the motion may be represented as follows:

Before the round, the adjudicator thought the motion was:

Throughout the course of the round, attentive adjudicators will listen to the arguments made by the various debaters, assess the quality of the arguments presented, evaluate the debaters' presentation of those arguments, and react to the effort of the debaters to execute a particular strategy in the debate. Following the round and after consideration of all these factors, the adjudicators' convictions may have shifted:

After the round, the adjudicator thought the motion was:

In this case, though the adjudicator continues to believe that the motion is true, the teams on the Opposition side would be more likely to win because they *moved* the adjudicator's conviction the farthest. Even though the adjudicators' opinion is that the motion is likely true, the Opposition team were successful in tempering that conviction. Though they didn't absolutely convince the adjudicators that the motion was false, they did affect the adjudicators more than did the Proposition teams.

The strength of this model is that it marries content (matter) to effort (manner) and is perfectly suited to Worlds-style debating, wherein each team must be evaluated for its contribution to the debate. The model also accounts for biases the adjudicator may possess and is capable of rewarding teams that challenge those biases even if they're unsuccessful at fully convincing an adjudicator of their position.

Relevant Standards of Adjudication

Adjudicators who specialize in Worlds-style debating employ a variety of standards to determine who wins the rounds, three of which are most common. None of these standards is definitive and each has its own strengths and weaknesses. Most importantly, these standards are best used in combination to produce a holistic assessment of the round.

ROLE FULFILLMENT

A common standard on the BP circuit is to evaluate each team's merit by assessing whether that team's speakers met the expectations of their respective roles. In a debate format that involves four teams competing independently of each other—but requiring cooperation with at least one other team—it's not surprising that adjudicators would have expectations regarding the contributions of each of the teams (and each speaker on those teams). Those expectations impart a certain structure and predictability to what may otherwise be a chaotic jangling of voices.

Although I will not repeat the detailed discussion of roles and responsibilities of each team member presented in Chapter 5, it is worth remembering the general charge of each. The first speaker positions for each opening team (the Prime Minister and the Leader Opposition) are responsible for setting their bench's direction. They outline both the interpretation of the motion and the team line that will guide the later speakers' efforts. Certainly their partners, and to a lesser but equally important extent their colleagues in the closing positions, have a responsibility to honor the direction set by their opening speaker. Thus, the opening speakers are generally evaluated most heavily on whether they start the debate off in the right direction.

The second speakers on the opening teams (the Deputy Prime Minister and the Deputy Leader Opposition) have not only the general charge of supporting their leader but the unique responsibility for thoroughly deconstructing the effort of the opposing team—the DPM because it's the first and only time the Opening Proposition team will get a shot at the Opening Opposition's constructive arguments and the DLO because it's the last time the adjudicators will hear from the Opening Opposition team.

The Member speakers (the Member of the Proposition and the Member of the Opposition) are primarily responsible for offering the Closing teams' extension in the round. To reinforce the "competing and cooperating" relationship between teams on the same benches, requires the Member speakers to identify a base of support for the direction offered by the Opening team while simultaneously distinguishing themselves from that team.

The Whip speakers (the Proposition Whip and the Opposition Whip) have the unique responsibility of summarizing the round for their respective sides. The ability to consider all the arguments in the round while promoting their side of the debate and, all the while, attempting to represent their arguments as the most significant in the round is a challenging task.

Some are legitimately concerned about an overemphasis of role fulfillment as a criterion employed by some adjudicators. It's true that novice adjudicators, particularly, are prone to a "tick the box" approach to adjudication and that the duties of each role provide a tempting list of expectations against which a speaker's efforts may be measured. The best adjudicators, however, limit their evaluation of a round with role fulfillment; they recognize that the satisfaction of role obligations is an important but singular aspect of successful debating. Such adjudicators also recognize that role expectations are not ends in themselves but merely the means by which to ensure the functionality of the round.

If the round thoroughly tests the proposition before the house, but the speakers do so without fulfilling their "traditional roles," an excellent adjudicator will reward those teams and speakers regardless of their deviation from the expectations of their roles.

THE "BETTER DEBATE" STANDARD

Not many adjudicators would refer to this standard as the "better debate" standard, but I have little doubt that many adjudicators employ the criteria that are foundational for this standard.

Phrased simply, the "better debate" standard asks, "Which team contributed most to (or detracted most from) the quality of this debate?" In other words, adjudicators using this standard ask themselves what each team did to make this debate *better*.

If this standard implies that adjudicators have in mind some Platonic form of the ideal debate, such an implication wouldn't be entirely inaccurate. Whether that form is based on an amalgam of the best debates the judges have witnessed or is the product of the adjudicators' more objective perspective about the appropriate focus of the round, the "perfect debate" is a standard against which many adjudicators evaluate debates.

In an effort to bring some objectivity to this standard, I recommend that adjudicators focus on four criteria to determine who most contributed to the quality of the round:

> *Inquiry*: Do the teams interrogate the most germane issues in the round?

> *Advancement*: Does each speech/speaker move the debate forward with new perspectives, arguments, or evidence?

Focus: Do the teams avoid distractions and concentrate their efforts on the most substantive issues in the round?

Performance: Do the teams deliver a compelling oratorical effort?

These four factors allow a more structured and impartial means by which to determine which team has done the most to make the debate better. The teams that contribute the most in each of these areas are typically those who make the debate better by moving it closer to the ideal debate round. Conversely, those who fail in these areas often detract from the overall quality of the round.

The better debate standard also implies that the best course of strategy isn't always the easy course. As noted in Chapter 7, the natural inclination of debaters to attempt to define the debate in terms most favorable to them may not produce the best debate.[54] The best debate is typically one that has ample ground for both sides, ground that allows each side to completely interrogate the full range of issues implied by the motion (or at least those issues that may potentially arise). Debaters would do well to keep in mind that the best debate for them (i.e., that which presents them with the most narrow, defensible ground) is rarely the best debate from the viewpoint of the adjudicators (i.e., that which presents the most ground for the proposition to be thoroughly tested).

MATTER AND MANNER

Matter and manner are the customary standards on which BP rounds are adjudicated. Codified in the Universities Debating Championship's "World Parliamentary Debating Rules," these criteria serve as a general expression of the most basic factors on which adjudicators should render a decision. As expressed in those rules, matter and manner are defined as follows:

Matter

3.1.1 Matter is the content of the speech. It is the arguments a debater uses to further his or her case and persuade the audience.
3.1.2 Matter includes arguments and reasoning, examples, case studies, facts and any other material that attempts to further the case.
3.1.3 Matter includes positive (or substantive) material and rebuttal (arguments specifically aimed to refute the arguments of the opposing team[s]). Matter includes Points of Information.

Manner

4.1.1 Manner is the presentation of the speech. It is the style and structure a member uses to further his or her case and persuade the audience.
4.1.2 Manner is comprised of many separate elements. Primarily, manner may be assessed by examining the speakers' style (delivery) and structure (organization).[55]

Armed with a general model of adjudication and having discussed some of the most common standards BP adjudicators use, we can now turn our attention to outlining the process of rendering a decision following a round.

Reaching a Decision

To reach a decision about which team should be ranked first, second, third, and fourth, the adjudicators must sort through and evaluate the competing lines of argument made by each of the four teams. Comparing the arguments of the debater that spoke in the first 7 minutes of a debate round to those made by the debater who spoke in the last 7 is a challenging task. In this section, I outline an approach that gives structure and direction to that process.

Comparing the relative efforts of teams in a debate round requires that adjudicators progress through six steps:

1. Identify the proposition
2. Identify the issues
3. Determine the winner of each issue
4. Determine the importance of each issue
5. Assess each team's effort relative to the issues
6. Justify and report the decision

To outline a plan for the evaluation of competing lines of argument, I'll treat each of these steps in order.[56]

1. IDENTIFY THE PROPOSITION

In Chapter 4, I discussed the nature and function of points of stasis in a debate. To the list of benefits derived from clearly identified points of stasis I should add that clearly identified and articulated points of stasis allow adjudicators to more accurately and thoroughly evaluate each team's effort. By first identifying the places where each team's arguments clashed with their opponents, the adjudicator will be better able to assess the relative merits of each team's arguments.

The first point of stasis the adjudicator should identify is the primary point of stasis in the round: the proposition. As noted earlier, the proposition is the major dividing line between the Proposition and Opposition sides in the round and functions as the dividing line in the ground over which the Proposition and Opposition disagree.

Propositions may either come from the motion provided to the teams or they may emerge from the arguments made in that round. If the motion is very straightforward, the motion itself may serve as the proposition for the round. The motion "This house would recognize the independence of Abkhazia" defines clear ground for the Proposition and Opposition and, therefore, would likely serve as the proposition. Other motions, such as "This house believes that religious leaders should listen to public opinion," provide less clear direction to the teams. These motions rely on the teams to negotiate the proposition in the round. For example, the Opening Proposition could choose to run a case that argues the Catholic Church should be more proactive in acknowledging and addressing issues of sexual abuse of minors by Catholic priests. When the Proposition chooses to define a case that is more focused and specific than the motion offered, and when the Opposition accepts that case as the focus of the debate, that interpretation becomes the proposition for the round.

While the proposition will usually be explicit in the round, there will be cases in which neither side makes clear the central focus in the round. In this case, the adjudicator must phrase a proposition that functions as the central point of stasis. This effort is a starting point for her adjudication and will later serve as a touchstone used to assess the arguments made by the teams.

When creating a proposition, an adjudicator should phrase a statement that is clear and balanced. To be clear, a proposition statement should define ground for both the Government and Opposition team in a way that makes obvious their responsibilities. A balanced proposition statement will avoid expressing the controversy in a way that might be weighted toward one side or the other.

2. IDENTIFY THE ISSUES

While each debate is defined by the proposition that divides the ground between the Proposition and Opposition, more specific points of stasis will emerge as the debate progresses. Known as issues, these minor points of stasis are those places where the particular arguments of each team interact with the responses of the opposing teams.

Issues emerge as the round progresses. They may come from the explicit efforts of the debaters; in an ideal situation, the debaters on both sides agree on the relevant issues in the round. In certain rounds, all four teams—explicitly or implicitly—may agree to structure their arguments around those issues. Unfortunately, in most cases the teams in a debate do not identify the issues so clearly. When the teams fail to do so, adjudicators must sift through the arguments offered by each team, attempt to phrase reasonable issue statements that are material to the proposition and inclusive of the arguments made by the teams, and, finally, to evaluate the various arguments made relative to these issues.

Consider a round on a motion that was popular a few years ago: "The United States should sever all ties with Pakistan's Musharraf regime." In this debate, the Opening Proposition forwarded a case focused primarily on the U.S. stated foreign policy goal of democratization of Middle Eastern nations. They then proceeded to identify how Pervez Musharraf has taken action to confound the democratic process and how the continued U.S. alliance with his administration condemns the United States to hypocrisy. The Opening Opposition countered that the Global War on Terror demands regional allies in the Middle East and

South Asia, and Musharraf, for his faults, has been a reliable partner in this war. The Closing Proposition offered an extension focusing on how withdrawing our support from Musharraf would force him to develop a power-sharing arrangement with former Pakistani Prime Minister Benazir Bhutto and that this coalition would settle the political tension in Pakistan. Closing Opposition disagreed and extended with an argument contending that withdrawing support from Musharraf would only force him to find other bases of power by tolerating a growing Islamic fundamentalist movement in northern Pakistan.

While the teams in this debate didn't explicitly identify the issues they were contesting, the adjudicators recognized themes in the arguments exchanged between teams. To organize their consideration of the arguments made in the round, the adjudicators framed three issues around which to consider the various arguments made by each team. Those issues included:

1. What foreign policy goals guide the United States in its formation of alliances?
2. Has the U.S. alliance with Musharraf advanced or hindered those goals?
3. What will happen if the United States withdraws its support from Musharraf?

These issue statements were valuable because they were inclusive of all the arguments made by the teams in the round. More to the point, these are the issues material to determining the truth or falsity of the motion. Notice, too, that there is a logical progressivity in the order of the issues: before the adjudicators could evaluate the U.S. alliance with Musharraf relative to our foreign policy goals, they first had to resolve what those goals were. Once they were able to determine whether the U.S. alliance helped or hindered those goals, the adjudicators were able to turn their attention to the question of the likely outcome of a withdrawal of support. This progressivity is the natural outcome of a rational, linear approach to decision making; adjudicators should seek to order the issues in a debate in a logical fashion when considering the arguments made by the teams.

3. DETERMINE THE WINNER OF EACH ISSUE

Once the adjudicators have identified the round's proposition and the issues relevant to that proposition have been identified, the real work of adjudication begins. The adjudicators must now determine which side prevailed in capturing ground on each issue. To do so, the adjudicators must assess the arguments of each team and the interaction of each team's arguments with the arguments made by other teams in the round.

While determining which team's arguments prevailed is a complex and subjective exercise, a couple of points will make this process easier: first, if the former two steps have been completed properly, the adjudicators can easily recognize where (i.e., over which issues) the teams' arguments compete. This clear structure is essential to determining which arguments prevail: to know which argument on either side of a common point wins, you must first know which issues are in contest.

After structuring the arguments so they are clearly opposed to each other, the adjudicators must then assess the merits of each team's argument relative to each issue. Again, while determining which argument you personally find most compelling is an inherently subjective process, the effort may be guided by traditional standards of argument quality: *truth* and *validity*.

Truth

The standard of truth asks, "Which side's arguments are most be-lievable?" To evaluate an argument's believability, an adjudicator may assess that argument's fidelity and coherence.

Fidelity refers to the arguments maintenance of external consisten-cy. Put simply, an argument maintains external consistency if it is con-sistent with what the adjudicator knows to be true. This is, of course, another way of asking if a particular claim is grounded in evidence that the judge finds acceptable; judges are more likely to believe claims sup-ported by such evidence. This is not to say that adjudicators automati-cally reject claims counter to what they believe is true, simply that adju-dicators — like all human beings — are more skeptical of that which does not mesh with their perception of what's right, true, and accurate.

Coherence, on the other hand, refers to an argument's maintenance of internal consistency. Internal consistency is maintained if an argument is not contradicted by some other argument made by the same team. Obvi-ously, a coherent strategy is essential to a successful effort; the presence of contradictions between a team's arguments is cause for concern.

Validity

To evaluate an argument's validity, the adjudicator must look to how a team conveys an argument. In the terms of formal logic, validity refers to the structure of an argument; if the premises and conclusion of an argument conform to a recognized (and logical) pattern, that argu-ment is judged to be valid. In more informal terms (and in terms more relevant to the evaluation of arguments in a competitive debate), an adjudicator may evaluate validity by examining the team's *execution* and *expression* of that argument.

Execution refers to the reasoning used to connect the claim to the evidence offered. If the debater's reasoning makes the support offered relevant to the claim advanced, the argument may be said to be valid. In more holistic terms, an adjudicator may also look to the function of that argument in the team's broader strategy. If a particular argument makes a significant and necessary contribution to a team's strategy, or if that strategy is particularly compelling relative to the proposition, the team executed the argument well.

Another way to judge the validity of an argument is to assess the debater's *expression* of that argument. The force of an argument is a product of both its content and its expression; an argument that is well-structured and conveyed passionately will necessarily garner more attention than one that is poorly organized or presented with little enthusiasm.

These criteria allow adjudicators to assess the relative power of each side's arguments and decide which side prevailed on each issue. Once the adjudicators know which side won each issue, they must determine the relative importance of that issue to the proposition being debated.

4. DETERMINE THE IMPORTANCE OF EACH ISSUE

Once the adjudicators reach a determination about which side won each issue, they can then evaluate the relative significance of each issue. As discussed in Chapter 3, any issue can be won by either the Proposition or the Opposition (represented below by the horizontal movement of the dividing line in an issue) and that same issue may occupy relatively more or less of the adjudicators' attention than other issues (represented by the vertical expansion of issues relative to each other).

To determine the relative importance of each issue, the adjudicators must return to the proposition around which the issues are focused. They may ask themselves which issues are most germane to the proposition at hand, giving greater weight to issues that more directly address the question and less to those issues deemed ancillary to the proposition. This is not, obviously, an exact science. Determining which issues are most significant requires the evaluation of a variety of factors, including assessing which are most relevant to the motion being debated, which issues the debaters claim are most important, and how each issue relates to the overall strategy of each team.

At the conclusion of this process, the adjudicators should have a clear picture of which side (Proposition or Opposition) won each issue and how significant those issues are to the proposition under consideration. At the end of our hypothetical debate on banning tobacco in Chapter 3, the "territory" of the round was divided like this:

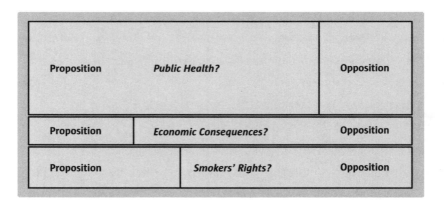

Based on the adjudicators' consideration of the issues in the round, it is clear that while the Opposition proved there would be economic consequences and a violation of smokers' rights if tobacco products were banned, the adjudicators were convinced that the issue of public health — clearly won by the Proposition side — was the most significant issue in the round.

5. ASSESS EACH TEAM'S EFFORTS RELATIVE TO THE ISSUES

In BP debating, unlike other formats of debate, simply determining which side prevailed on the proposition does not automatically determine who won the round. The BP format requires that adjudicators decide which team should be ranked first, second, third, and fourth in the round. Adding to that complication is that in BP debating there is no recognition of a winning "side." There exists the very real possibility that teams from opposing sides may be ranked in ways that don't make either side the clear victor: it is not only likely but typical that the Opening Proposition would be ranked first, the Opening Opposition ranked second, the Closing Opposition ranked third, and the Closing Proposition team ranked fourth. In such a scenario, both "sides" have received an equal number of points, thereby not indicating a "win" for either side. Because teams in a BP round receive ordinal rankings, determining the winning side is never enough. An adjudicator must also determine which teams contributed most significantly to the overall effort in the round.

Another way to express this, consistent with the "mental map" metaphor used throughout this book, is that the winning team is the one that occupies the majority of the adjudicators' attention at the end of the round. The second place team is the team that occupies the second most attention, and so on. Fortunately, the map metaphor may be adapted easily to this assessment. In addition to representing which side won each issue and the relative significance of each issue, the territory of the debate may be mapped to represent each team's contribution to that effort:

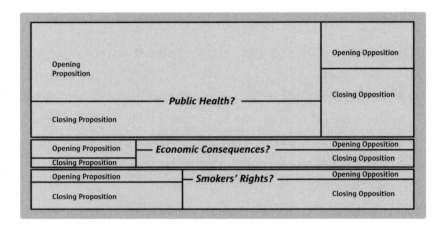

According to the map of this round's territory, at the end of this round, the Opening Proposition team would be ranked first, since they not only were on the winning side of the most critical issue, but in the adjudicators' assessment they were most responsible for proving that public health would benefit from a ban on tobacco. On the other issues—though ultimately the adjudicators' felt the Opposition side prevailed on both less important issues—the Opening Proposition team made the greatest contribution to the overall Proposition effort on the economic consequences issue and a lesser contribution to the issue of smokers' rights. In any case, as the map represents, the Opening Proposition's arguments occupy the majority of territory in the adjudicators' consideration of the round.

The adjudicators would rank the Closing Opposition team second. They were responsible for whatever successes the Opposition side enjoyed as represented by the fact that their arguments occupy the second most ground in the adjudicators' consideration of the round. Even though their side lost the debate, they were clearly responsible for the bulk of the compelling arguments about all three issues (and, the adjudicators won't likely forget, won two of the three issues).

The Closing Proposition would likely be ranked third, given their support of the winning side of the critical issue and that they at least contributed most to the Proposition's effort on the smokers' rights issue. Though they didn't accomplish as much as the Closing Opposition, they do — in the end — occupy more space in the mind of the adjudicators than the Opening Opposition, which, given their minimal contribution to the Opposition's effort in all the issues in the debate, would be ranked last.

6. REPORT THE DECISION

The final responsibility of the adjudicators is to report their decision. An effective oral adjudication is critical to good judging. The oral adjudication presents the adjudicators the opportunity to explain how they interpreted the round and to meet their obligation to the principle of education discussed earlier. If an adjudicator has progressed through the steps as outlined, an effective oral adjudication should be easy.

I recommend using the steps as the structure for the oral adjudication. Begin by identifying the proposition. You'll want to explain how you arrived at that proposition, either from the motion, the teams' interpretation of that motion, or by your own assessment of the general point of focus for the teams' arguments. From there, you should identify the issues that you believe were contested between the teams by pointing to specific arguments that were made for and against that issue.

The next three steps in the judging process are usually combined. The topics of which team won each issue, how important each issue was relative to the other issues, and which team made the greatest contribution to the effort to prove or disprove an issue are typically presented in concert with extensive references to specific arguments the teams made. At times, the same argument that wins an issue simultaneously proves that issue is most important. Identifying the debater (or team) responsible for making that argument is likely the way in which the adjudicators will highlight the argument that most affected their decision.

At the end of the day, the judges must render a decision and present a rationale for that decision that is mindful of the guiding principles of adjudication discussed above. Their decision should adhere to the movement model and present a good faith effort to consider all the arguments made by each team and the relative merit of those arguments. When done well, the adjudicators' contribution is a satisfying accompaniment to the intellectual efforts of the debaters.

NOTES

1. Burke, Kenneth, and Joseph R. Gusfield. 1989. *On symbols and society*. Chicago: University of Chicago Press.

2. Berger, Charles R., and Richard J. Calabrese. 1975. Some explorations in initial interaction and beyond: Toward a developmental theory of interpersonal communication. *Human Communication Research* 1 (2, Winter): 99.

3. Foucault, Michel. 1972. *The archaeology of knowledge*. Trans. A. M. Sheridan Smith. New York: Pantheon.

4. This is, of course, a dramatic oversimplification of the process. Rarely are the constraints of public discourse as clear as they are in a debate round; rarely does public discourse ever come to as clear and final an end as the adjudication that punctuates a debate round. That notwithstanding — and recognizing that even when the "majority" opinion has been formed, there still may exist a strong and vocal "minority" opinion — this provides a useful explanation of the role of argument in the formation of collective understanding.

5. Of course, the list of "allowed" techniques and tactics is governed by ethical limits inherent in all human interaction: honesty, good faith, tolerance, nonviolence, and many other values govern our persuasive efforts outside of a debate round. These limits should not be left at the door of the debating chamber.

6. Trapp, Robert, and William Driscoll. 2005. *Discovering the world through debate: A practical guide to educational debate for debaters, coaches and judges*. 3rd ed. New York: International Debate Education Association.

7. Relational argumentation, according to Trapp, may also address relationships of similarity wherein the arguer attempts to demonstrate the likeness (or unlikeness) of things. I would add that argumentation concerning coexistential relationships — arguments that assert that two (or more) things exist simultaneously and in relation to each other — should also be included in this mode of argument. As Trapp notes, however, none of these relationships is of as great a concern to the debater as causal relationships.

8. Incidentally, these scientists would similarly be relying on arguments to establish the likelihood of their causal claims. The scientific method is based upon the assertion of a (usually) causal relationship, the collection of evidence that demonstrates the existence of that relationship, and, finally, the interpretation of that evidence through the construction of arguments about the meaning of the evidence.

9. Lakoff, George, and Mark Johnson. 1980. *Metaphors we live by*. Chicago: University of Chicago Press.

10. Certainly there is some strategic consideration to the ordering of issues — the principle of primacy and recency, for example, suggests that when presenting issues, you should treat those most critical to your success either first or last, as they are more likely to attract the

attention of your audience in those positions. There is no logical relationship between these issues, however.

11. Here's a good place to note that to separate an argument's structure from its substance is impossible: the substance of an argument IS how it is structured; the structure of an argument IS the substance of that argument. What distinguishes an argument from other forms of thought (feelings, impressions, intuitions, etc.) is that an argument expresses a particular relationship between ideas; one cannot be separated from the other. That said, there is some clarity that may be gained from pretending that this distinction is possible.

12. See, for example, Aristotle's discussion of *topoi* in *The Rhetoric* (Aristotle. 1991. *The art of rhetoric*. New York: Penguin Books) and Perelman and Olbrechts-Tyteca's consideration of *loci* in *The New Rhetoric* (Perelman, Chaïm, and Lucie Olbrechts-Tyteca. 1969. *The new rhetoric: A treatise on argumentation*. Notre Dame, IN: University of Notre Dame Press).

13. For a brief introduction to Gestalt psychology, see Richards, Graham. 1996. *Putting psychology in its place: An introduction from a critical historical perspective*. New York: Routledge.

14. Trapp's discussion of the acceptability, relevance, and sufficiency standards in *Discovering the World through Debate* draws upon the work of Johnson and J. Anthony Blair in *Logical Self Defense* (Johnson, Ralph H., and J. Anthony Blair. 1994. *Logical self defense*. New York: McGraw-Hill) and Govier's *A Practical Study of Argument* (Govier, Trudy. 2001. *A practical study of argument*. Belmont, CA: Wadsworth).

15. For a more thorough discussion of these types of reasoning and the tests of each type (i.e., the determination of the *relevance* of the relationship between claim and evidence, see Trapp, Chapter 5).

16. In his discussion of the sufficiency standard, Trapp refers to the varying levels of proof required by different aspects of the American justice system. In the American criminal system, generally an argument must be proved "beyond a reasonable doubt" to be accepted. In America's civil courts, on the other hand, an argument that proves a preponderance of the evidence (or 51% certainty) lies with a particular side will be accepted. Trapp also observes that sufficiency is tied to the consequences of accepting and rejecting the argument presented. An argument with more dramatic consequences ("we should act now to stop global climate change") may require a lower standard of sufficiency than an argument that produces less drastic consequences, merely because the risk of not accepting such an argument is enormous. In the case of the global climate change example, a failure to accept the argument and, therefore, act, potentially subjects us to the most extreme consequences of environmental collapse.

17. Goodnight, G. Thomas. 1982. The personal, technical, and public spheres of argument: A speculative inquiry into the art of public deliberation. *Journal of the American Forensics Association* 18 (4, Spring): 214.

18. See the discussion in Chapter 2 regarding the occupation of psychological "space" in the mind of the judge.

19. See the discussion of *propositions* and *issues* in Chapter 3.

20. For more on why arguments must be grouped together, please review the discussion of points of stasis, and issues in particular, in Chapter 3.

21. Hayakawa, S. I., and Alan R. Hayakawa. 1990. *Language in thought and action.* 5th ed. San Diego, Calif.: Harcourt Brace Jovanovich.

22. I first heard John Meany, director of debate at Claremont McKenna Colleges, use this analogy at a training session for debaters new to the BP style at a tournament hosted by Claremont Colleges in October 2005. Meany and Kate Schuster also employ this analogy in their 2002 text *Art, Argument and Advocacy* (Meany, John, and Kate Shuster. 2002. *Art, argument and advocacy: Mastering parliamentary debate.* New York: International Debate Education Association).

23. The term "model" is the prevalent name for this portion of the case on the informal circuit that competes in the BP format. Other academic debating formats — most notably the American policy debating community — call this portion of a case the "plan." Debates that occur in legislatures around the world typically discuss the proposed action being debated as a "policy" or a "proposal." All these things are functionally the same.

24. Please see Chapter 9 for a more complete discussion of the "better debate" standard.

25. For more discussion of what seems to be contradictory advice ("to be evaluated favorably, define the motion in a way that opens the door to Opposition arguments"), see my discussion of the fourth paradox of debate in Chapter 7.

26. Although even in this instance a good case can be made for the LO to merely acknowledge this error and then engage the Opening Proposition in the debate about corporal punishment. For the good of the debate — and to avoid rendering at least one-eighth, if not one-quarter, of the debate irrelevant — debating about making spanking illegal might be the LO's best choice.

27. See WUDC Rules: Part 2, Section 2.1.3 concerning the requirements of an acceptable interpretation of a motion (World universities debating championships rules. World Debating Web site. 2006 [cited February 9, 2009]. Available from http://flynn.debating.net/Colm-main_wudc.htm).

28. Of course, an option available to the LO is to object to the PM's definition, to offer a case arguing against the "correct" interpretation of the motion, and then to argue against the incorrect interpretation promulgated by the Opening Proposition. Any successful general will tell you, though, that few wars fought on two fronts are successful. More to the point, by engaging the "incorrect," interpretation the LO risks lending it legitimacy merely by the act of paying attention to it. Choose carefully.

29. WUDC Rules: Part 2, Section 2.3.

30. WUDC Rules: Part 3, Section 3.2.5.

31. See the discussion of the function of propositions and issues in Chapter 3 and the discussion of evaluating issues relative to the proposition in Chapter 9.

32. Here is a good place to remind the reader that the most useful chapter in this book is the

one on how to adjudicate a debate. Debaters who want to know how to win a debate round should first know how adjudicators think.

33. Baron, Jonathan. 2000. *Thinking and deciding*. 3rd ed. Cambridge, UK: Cambridge University Press, 5.

34. Baron, 6.

35. Baron, 15.

36. Baron, 8.

37. Baron's characterization of the motive for thinking corresponds nicely with the discussion of the motivating force of "uncertainty" as discussed in Chapter 1. In both cases, anxiety about the unknown prompts some cognitive effort.

38. As discussed in Chapter 5, the best choice in this case was the broadest definition. This option not only mirrors current practice as it exists in competitive BP debating but also most clearly satisfies the "better debate" standard used by many adjudicators when determining rankings in the round.

39. Baron, 9.

40. This is not the exclusive source of goals that may weigh in the adjudicators' decision. As noted earlier, Baron argues that the elements discovered in the search process may come from two sources: external sources — such as those advocated by the debaters in the round — and internally from the decision maker him- or herself. In other words, the adjudicator may bring to the round his or her own conception of goals relevant to the decision he or she will make. Many an adjudicator has frustrated (or educated) a debater with a comment like "you missed a relevant point in the debate by ignoring X" where "X" was the goal the adjudicator thought was important (but was unaddressed in the debate). Debaters can mitigate this in two ways: first, they must thoroughly analyze each proposition to uncover and address all the goals in the goals system relevant to the decision-making process. Second, the debaters should do their best to be aware of any contextual cues relevant to determining what the adjudicators will find important: review the discussion of value systems to reflect upon which cues will help you to make this determination.

41. Of course, fuel efficiency has benefits beyond the money one saves. The environmental impact of consuming less fossil-based fuel may be the main concern of the purchaser, in which case the goal of affordability would not subsume fuel efficiency.

42. Rokeach, Milton. 1973. *The nature of human values*. New York: Free Press.

43. Foulk, T. Griffith. 2000. The form and function of koan literature: A historical overview. In *The koan: Texts and contexts in Zen Buddhism*, eds. Steven Heine and Dale Stuart Wright, 322. Oxford, UK: Oxford University Press.

44. For more on using goals to guide your strategic choices, see the section in Chapter 8 about "goal analysis."

45. For more on using presumption to empower your arguments, see the discussion of offensive tactics in Chapter 8.

46. See Chapter 9 for more discussion of how the "better debate" standard operates as a criterion for adjudication.

47. WUDC Rules: Part 2, Section 2.1.3.

48. Whately, Richard. 1963. Elements of rhetoric. Carbondale: Southern Illinois University Press.

49. World Medical Association. 1968. World medical association declaration of Helsinki: Ethical principles for medical research involving human subjects. Helsinki. Available from http://www.wma.net/e/policy/b3.htm.

50. There are a variety of ways to determine what your adjudicator(s) believe: for example, you can make generalizations from their demographic characteristics, you may ask other teams, and you may rely on previous instances in which they served as adjudicators in your rounds.

51. Bitzer, Lloyd F. 1968. The rhetorical situation. *Philosophy and Rhetoric* 1, (1, Winter): 1.

52. It should be obvious at this point that implicit collusion is an option that may be exercised most effectively by the closing teams. The team in the Opening Proposition position has little choice about the team with whom they develop a strategic correlationship; as no team other than the Opening Opposition will present their arguments before the Opening Proposition finishes speaking, it is the Opening Opposition that the Opening Proposition must engage. That said, there are subtle ways of utilizing this tactic even for those teams in the opening positions; those ways are discussed in the section on "implementing the correlationship."

53. In particular, the *Guide to Chairing and Adjudicating a Worlds Debate,* adopted by the World Universities Debating Council, is a very thorough introduction to the administration of a Worlds-style round (Abdullah, Omar S., Ian Lising, Steven L. Johnson and Ray D'Cruz. *Guide to chairing and adjudicating a worlds debate.* World Debating Website. 2005 [cited February 9, 2009]. Available from http://flynn.debating.net/omarguide.htm.).

54. See the discussion of Paradox #4 in Chapter 7.

55. WUDC Rules: Parts 3 and 4.

56. This section draws heavily from my writing for *Section 6: Evaluating Competing Lines of Argument* of the *Guide to Chairing and Adjudicating a Worlds Debate.*